WRITING BETTER ENGLISH

AN ESL WORKBOOK

Ed Swick

McGraw-Hill

New York Chicago San Francisco Lisbon London Madrid Mexico City Milan New Delhi San Juan Seoul Singapore Sydney Toronto

The McGraw-Hill Companies

5 6 7 8 9 0 QPD/QPD 3 2 1 0 9 8 7

ISBN 0-07-142643-4

Interior design by Nick Panos

McGraw-Hill books are available at special quantity discounts to use as premiums and sales promotions, or for use in corporate training programs. For more information, please write to the Director of Special Sales, Professional Publishing, McGraw-Hill, Two Penn Plaza, New York, NY 10121-2298. Or contact your local bookstore.

This book is printed on acid-free paper.

Contents

Introduction

Writing in any language is a difficult skill to acquire. Therefore, as an ESL student you should approach writing in English carefully. In order to write well, you want to first have an understanding of grammatical structures, vocabulary, and tense usage. You practice those concepts until you can use them with relative ease. Then you are ready to practice writing original material.

This book does two things:

1. It gives you an abundant review of basic structures.
2. It provides various forms of writing practice within a controlled program that focuses on improving the skills needed to write accurately.

In Chapter 1 you will have the opportunity to learn or review grammar basics. By checking the Answer Key at the end of this book, you can find the correct or example answers to the exercises. If you have an English-speaking friend, you might ask him or her to check your work.

If you wish, you can follow your progress by using a very simple method. After each exercise, count every word that you have written—even little words like *the*, *a*, *and*, or *but*. Then count every error you have made in spelling, tense, word order, missing words, or any other potential mistake.

Divide the number of words you have written (W) by the number of errors (E) you have made. The result is a number (N) that you can compare after every exercise you write:

W ÷ E = N

If you wrote sixty words and made twelve errors, you would come up with:

60 ÷ 12 = 5

If the number is getting larger, you are making progress.

After completing the review exercises, you will be ready to begin Chapter 2. In this chapter you will complete sentences with your original phrases, and you will use your own ideas as you write. You will see a sentence similar to this:

John borrowed ____________________ to get to work.

You might write something like this:

John borrowed *his father's new car* to get to work.

For each exercise in Chapter 3 you will compose ten short, original sentences while using a phrase as the specific element in each sentence. For example:

Sample phrase: The new car
Used as the subject: The new car is in the garage.
Used as the direct object: Mary loved the new car.
Used after the preposition *to*: A man came up to the new car.

You may, of course, use dictionaries and grammar books as aids in order to write as correctly as possible. You could give yourself a time limit (fifteen minutes or thirty minutes) for writing the exercise, but use the same number of minutes each time you write.

In Chapter 4 you will fill in the missing phrases or sentences in a story. They can be any phrases or sentences that you wish, but they must conform to the plot of the story. For example:

The Diamond Ring

The robber crept into the hallway of the dark house and turned on the light. On the desk he saw a beautiful silver box holding a diamond ring, which he put in his pocket. Then he opened the window, jumped to the ground, and fled down the street.

Chapter 5 deals with letter writing. Each letter can be written within the same framework of time (fifteen minutes, thirty minutes, or longer). There is a difference between "friendly" letters and "business" letters. This part of the writing program will help you to write both types of letters.

In Chapter 6 you will write original stories. The stories are to be based on the assigned topic. and they should include the grammar structures indicated. For example:

> **Sample title:** Lost in the Desert
> **Include these structures:**
> the relative pronoun *which*
> *to want to* in the past perfect tense
> the conjunction *if*

You would then write a story about someone lost and roaming the desert. You would probably write of heat and thirst and of the difficulties of finding a way to safety. And somewhere in your story you would have three sentences similar to these (which include the required sample structures):

> She believed she saw a lake, **which**, unfortunately, was only a mirage.
> She **had** often **wanted to** climb a sand dune.
> **If** she found water, she knew she would survive.

If you feel you have not done well enough in any chapter of this book, do not go on to the next chapter. Instead, repeat the chapter that needs improvement. Set a standard of quality for yourself and conform to it. Use the Answer Key not only to check your work but also to find suggestions for how to write appropriate sentences for any of the exercises.

1

Preparing to Write

In order to write well in English, you should understand the basics of the language. Probably the most difficult area for students learning English is verbs. Although English verbs are used in complicated ways, they do not have complicated conjugations with a different ending for each pronoun like other languages might.

GERMAN	SPANISH	RUSSIAN
ich fahre	yo hablo	я играю
du fährst	tu hablas	ты играешь
er fährt	el habla	он играет
wir fahren	nosotros hablamos	мы играем
ihr fährt	vosotros habláis	вы играете
sie fahren	ellos hablan	они играют

With most English verbs there is only one ending (*-s* or *-es*) in the third person singular of the present tense. The only exception to that rule is the verb *to be*:

TO SPEAK	TO BE
I speak	I am
you speak	you are
he speaks	he is
we speak	we are
you speak	you are
they speak	they are

But English has other complexities. For example, there are three ways to express the present tense:

- The simple conjugation of the verb means that the *action of the verb is a habit or is repeated*. For example: "We speak."

- When the verb is conjugated with a form of *to be* (am, is, are, was, were), the verb will have an *-ing* ending. It means that the action is *continuing or not yet completed.* For example: "We are speaking."
- The third present tense form uses a conjugation of *to do* (do, does) with the verb and has three uses: (1) It is used to ask a question with most verbs except *to be* or certain auxiliaries (can, must, should, and so on). (2) It is used as an emphatic response. (3) It is used to negate the verb with *not.* Let's look at some examples with the verb *to speak*:

I speak English. (This is my habit. I speak English all the time.)
I am speaking English. (I usually speak Spanish. At the moment I am speaking English.)
Do you speak English? (A question with the verb *to speak.*)
I do speak English. (This is your emphatic response to someone who has just said, "You don't speak English.")
I do not speak English. (Negation of the verb *to speak* with *not.*)

Conjugating English verbs is not difficult. But choosing the correct tense form from the three just described requires practice. The exercises that follow will help you to use English verb forms and tenses with accuracy.

Verb Tenses

Study the following examples, which show how verbs change in the various tenses. Some tenses require a form of *to be* and a present participle. Present participles have an *-ing* ending: *is going, were singing.* Other tenses require a past participle. Regular verbs form the past tense and past participle in the same way—just add *-ed*: *worked, have worked.* Use the appendix of irregular verbs in the past tense and past participle to see how they are formed.

The perfect tenses of both regular and irregular verbs are a combination of a form of *to have* plus a past participle: *I have worked. She has seen. You had broken. Tom will have discovered.*

In the exercises that follow you will be making similar tense changes.

TO SPEAK—a habit or repeated action

Present	She speaks well.
Past	She spoke well.

Present Perfect	She has spoken well.
Past Perfect	She had spoken well.
Future	She will speak well.
Future Perfect	She will have spoken well.

TO BE SPEAKING—a continuous action

Present	Who is speaking?
Past	Who was speaking?
Present Perfect	Who has been speaking?
Past Perfect	Who had been speaking?
Future	Who will be speaking?
Future Perfect	Who will have been speaking?

DO YOU SPEAK?—a question with a form of *to do*

Present	Do you speak Spanish?
Past	Did you speak Spanish?
Present Perfect	Have you spoken Spanish?
Past Perfect	Had you spoken Spanish?
Future	Will you speak Spanish?
Future Perfect	Will you have spoken Spanish?

(Because the perfect and future tenses in the preceding example have an auxiliary verb [have, had, will] in the question, a form of *to do* is not necessary.)

SHE DOESN'T SPEAK—negation of the verb with a form of *to do*

Present	She doesn't speak French.
Past	She didn't speak French.
Present Perfect	She hasn't spoken French.
Past Perfect	She hadn't spoken French.
Future	She won't speak French.
Future Perfect	She won't have spoken French.

(Because the perfect and future tenses in the preceding example have an auxiliary verb [hasn't, hadn't, won't] in the sentence, a form of *to do* is not necessary.)

Exercise 1.1 Rewrite the following sentences in the tenses given. Use the examples given previously to help you maintain accuracy.

1. Present *Her brother looks for us.*
   Past ______
   Past Perfect ______
   Future ______

2. Present ______
   Past *Were you looking for your wallet?*
   Present Perfect ______
   Past Perfect ______
   Future ______

3. Present ______
   Past ______
   Present Perfect ______
   Past Perfect ______
   Future *Will she help Tom?*

4. Present ______
   Past ______
   Present Perfect *I haven't filled out the application.*
   Past Perfect ______
   Future ______

5. Present *Do they play soccer?*
   Past ______
   Present Perfect ______
   Past Perfect ______
   Future ______

6. Present ______
   Past ______
   Present Perfect ______
   Past Perfect ______
   Future *He will be making a good salary.*

7. Present ______________________
   Past ______________________
   Present Perfect ______________________
   Past Perfect *Juan had visited his aunt and uncle.*
   Future ______________________
   Future Perfect ______________________

8. Present ______________________
   Past *She carried the child to her bed.*
   Present Perfect ______________________
   Past Perfect ______________________
   Future ______________________

9. Present *My sister often dates Michael.*
   Past ______________________
   Present Perfect ______________________
   Past Perfect ______________________
   Future ______________________

10. Present ______________________
    Past ______________________
    Present Perfect *They have hired him.*
    Past Perfect ______________________
    Future ______________________

Exercise 1.2 Rewrite the following sentences in the tenses given. Use the examples to help you maintain accuracy.

1. Present *Her brother is very rich.*
   Past ______________________
   Past Perfect ______________________
   Future ______________________

2. Present ______________________
   Past *Were the children good?*
   Present Perfect ______________________
   Past Perfect ______________________
   Future ______________________

3. Present ______________________________
   Past ______________________________
   Present Perfect ______________________________
   Past Perfect ______________________________
   Future *Will she be ill?*

4. Present ______________________________
   Past ______________________________
   Present Perfect *I have not been angry at all.*
   Past Perfect ______________________________
   Future ______________________________

5. Present *Do you go there often?*
   Past ______________________________
   Present Perfect ______________________________
   Past Perfect ______________________________
   Future ______________________________

6. Present ______________________________
   Past ______________________________
   Present Perfect ______________________________
   Past Perfect ______________________________
   Future *What will you do?*

7. Present ______________________________
   Past ______________________________
   Present Perfect ______________________________
   Past Perfect *The girls had had a bad day.*
   Future ______________________________
   Future Perfect ______________________________

8. Present ______________________________
   Past *Maria had ten dollars.*
   Present Perfect ______________________________
   Past Perfect ______________________________
   Future ______________________________

9. Present *My brother does nothing all day.*
   Past ______________________________
   Present Perfect ______________________________

Past Perfect ______________________________
Future ______________________________

10. Present ______________________________
Past ______________________________
Present Perfect *They haven't gone to the movies.*
Past Perfect ______________________________
Future ______________________________

Exercise 1.3 Rewrite the following sentences in the tenses given. Use the examples to help you maintain accuracy. Notice that you will be dealing with a wider variety of verbs here.

1. Present *Mark likes the new girl.*
Past ______________________________
Past Perfect ______________________________
Future ______________________________

2. Present *Her boss is trying to understand.*
Past ______________________________
Present Perfect ______________________________
Past Perfect ______________________________
Future ______________________________

3. Present ______________________________
Past *The letter carriers went into the office.*
Present Perfect ______________________________
Past Perfect ______________________________
Future ______________________________
Future Perfect ______________________________

4. Present ______________________________
Past *Were you talking to Richard?*
Present Perfect ______________________________
Past Perfect ______________________________
Future ______________________________

5. Present ______________________________
Past ______________________________
Present Perfect *His son has broken a window.*

Past Perfect ______________________________
Future ______________________________

6. Present ______________________________
Past ______________________________
Present Perfect *The secretary has been writing letters.*
Past Perfect ______________________________
Future ______________________________

7. Present ______________________________
Past ______________________________
Present Perfect ______________________________
Past Perfect ______________________________
Future *Won't you sing, too?*

8. Present ______________________________
Past ______________________________
Present Perfect ______________________________
Past Perfect ______________________________
Future *They won't be going shopping.*

9. Present ______________________________
Past ______________________________
Present Perfect ______________________________
Past Perfect ______________________________
Future ______________________________
Future Perfect *Carlos will have gotten up before dawn.*

10. Present ______________________________
Past ______________________________
Present Perfect ______________________________
Past Perfect ______________________________
Future ______________________________
Future Perfect *By seven-thirty he will have left for home.*

Exercise 1.4 Rewrite the following sentences in the tenses given, but change the subject of each sentence to a different pronoun (I, you, he, she, it, we, they, or who).

Present He sees you.
Past I saw you.
Present Perfect She has seen you.
Past Perfect They had seen you.
Future We will see you.

1. Present *Are you on time?*
   Past ______
   Present Perfect ______
   Past Perfect ______
   Future ______

2. Present ______
   Past *Didn't she like the book?*
   Past Perfect ______
   Future ______

3. Present ______
   Past ______
   Present Perfect *I have been driving very slowly.*
   Past Perfect ______
   Future ______

4. Present ______
   Past ______
   Present Perfect ______
   Past Perfect *We had found him just in time.*
   Future ______
   Future Perfect ______

5. Present ______
   Past ______
   Present Perfect ______
   Past Perfect ______

Future *They will arrange a party for her.*
Future Perfect ______

6. Present ______
Past ______
Present Perfect ______
Past Perfect ______
Future ______
Future Perfect *He will have brought it home by noon.*

7. Present *You eat too much.*
Past ______
Present Perfect ______
Past Perfect ______
Future ______

8. Present ______
Past *I put the tools back before lunch.*
Present Perfect ______
Past Perfect ______
Future ______
Future Perfect ______

9. Present *She cuts out the dress before bedtime.*
Past ______
Present Perfect ______
Past Perfect ______
Future ______
Future Perfect ______

10. Present ______
Past ______
Past Perfect ______
Future ______
Future Perfect *He will have stolen the money by midnight.*

You have been forming the future tense by using *will* with a verb (I will go, she will sing, they will be taking). The auxiliary *shall* is often used in the first person singular and plural (I and we). But in casual English *will* is used nearly all the time.

FORMAL	**CASUAL**
I shall visit my uncle.	I will visit my uncle.
We shall borrow some money.	We will borrow some money.

The future tense meaning is also expressed with the phrase *to be going to* (I am going to, you are going to, he is going to). It means the same thing as *will* and can replace it.

WILL	**TO BE GOING TO**
They will buy a new car.	They are going to buy a new car.
Will you help me?	Are you going to help me?

The phrase *to be going to* can be conjugated in the past tense. Then it means that this *was* something that someone *planned* to do in the future.

They were going to buy a new car.
Were you going to help me?

Exercise 1.5 Rewrite the following future tense sentences by changing *will* to *to be going to*.

1. Will they bring some dessert along?

____

2. I'll be home at midnight.

____

3. The janitor will sweep the offices after closing time.

____

4. He won't return the money he borrowed.

____

5. This movie will be very exciting.

____

6. The party will be held at Maria's house.

____

7. Will Martin apply for a new job?

____

8. She will probably spend the night at Mary's apartment.

____

9. Will you order a hamburger or a hot dog?

____

10. The boys will clean the kitchen for you.

____

Auxiliaries

It's very common to use *to have* or *to be* as auxiliaries or helping verbs. For example:

- Have you seen that film? (a form of *to have* plus a past participle)
- I haven't had a chance to go to the store today. (a form of *to have* plus a past participle)
- Are you learning a lot of new words? (a form of *to be* plus a present participle)
- She isn't studying for her exams. (a form of *to be* plus a present participle)

But there are other auxiliary verbs that are used with infinitives (to go, to run, to help, to find, and so on).

Note that many of these special verbs *cannot be used in all tenses.* And in some cases, you have to change to a *different* verb to form a specific tense. The examples that follow will be conjugated with the third person pronoun *he.*

	TO BE ABLE TO	**TO BE SUPPOSED TO**
Present	is able to	is supposed to
Past	was able to	was supposed to
Present Perfect	has been able to	has been supposed to
Past Perfect	had been able to	had been supposed to
Future	will be able to	will be supposed to
Future Perfect	will have been able to	will have been supposed to

	CAN	**TO HAVE TO**
Present	can	has to
Past	could *or* was able to	had to
Present Perfect	has been able to	has had to
Past Perfect	had been able to	had had to
Future	will be able to	will have to
Future Perfect	will have been able to	will have had to

	MAY	**MUST**
Present	may	must
Past	might	had to
Present Perfect	—	has had to
Past Perfect	—	had had to
Future	—	will have to
Future Perfect	—	will have had to

	OUGHT TO	**SHOULD**
Present	ought to	should
Past	—	—
Present Perfect	—	—
Past Perfect	—	—
Future	—	—
Future Perfect	—	—

	TO WANT	**TO NEED TO**
Present	wants	needs to
Past	wanted	needed to
Present Perfect	has wanted	has needed to
Past Perfect	had wanted	had needed to
Future	will want	will need to
Future Perfect	will have wanted	will have needed to

Exercise 1.6 Rewrite the following sentences in the tenses given. Use the preceding examples to help you maintain accuracy. Notice that these sentences contain auxiliaries, and remember that not all the tenses can be formed with some of these verbs.

1. Present *Can you hear me well enough?*
   Past ______
   Present Perfect ______
   Past Perfect ______
   Future ______

2. Present ______
   Past *Martin wanted to buy a car.*
   Present Perfect ______
   Past Perfect ______
   Future ______

3. Present ______
   Past *I was supposed to go home by eight o'clock.*
   Past Perfect ______

4. Present *May I try on your new coat?*
   Past ______

5. Present *She is not able to visit you today.*
   Past ______
   Present Perfect ______
   Past Perfect ______
   Future ______

6. Present ______
   Past ______
   Present Perfect *Have you had to study before the test?*
   Past Perfect ______
   Future ______
   Future Perfect ______

7. Present *The youngest children shouldn't stay out late.*
   Past ______
   Present Perfect ______

Past Perfect ______________________________

Future ______________________________

8. Present *You ought to sell that old bike.*

Past ______________________________

Present Perfect ______________________________

Past Perfect ______________________________

Future ______________________________

Future Perfect ______________________________

9. Present *Juan must work all day.*

Past ______________________________

Present Perfect ______________________________

Past Perfect ______________________________

Future ______________________________

Future Perfect ______________________________

10. Present ______________________________

Past ______________________________

Present Perfect ______________________________

Past Perfect *She hadn't needed to get there on time.*

Future ______________________________

Auxiliaries are followed by a verb in its infinitive form minus the particle word *to*. Look at these examples with the infinitive *to work*.

able to work	ought to work	can work
have to work	supposed to work	must work
need to work		may work
want to work		should work

When you use one of the auxiliaries with a verb, you tell *to what degree of obligation* someone has to carry out the action of the verb. Look at the following sentences. The first one shows the *least degree of obligation*. This is something someone doesn't have to do. The last sentence shows the *greatest degree of obligation*. This is something that someone absolutely must do.

We may return the books. (Least obligation. It's our choice.)
We can return the books. (Little obligation. It's our choice.)

We are able to return the books. (Little obligation. We have the ability to do this.)
We need to return the books. (Slight obligation.)
We ought to return the books. (Little obligation. But this would be a good idea.)
We should return the books. (Little obligation. But this would be a good idea.)
We are supposed to return the books. (Some obligation. Someone has suggested we do this.)
We must return the books. (Greatest obligation. It is our duty to do this.)
We have to return the books. (Greatest obligation. It is our duty to do this.)

When you add an auxiliary to a sentence, you should use the same tense as the original verb. For example: "John found [past tense] a good book." When you add *have to* to that sentence, you say, "John had to [past tense] find a good book."

Exercise 1.7 Rewrite the following sentences with the auxiliaries given. Be sure to retain the same tense as in the original sentence.

1. James borrows a book from Maria. (*to want to*)

___

2. I found some extra money. (*to need to*)

___

3. Mr. Sanchez leaves his luggage at the door. (*must*)

___

4. Did you already speak English as a child? (*can*)

___

5. We haven't written the whole assignment. (*to be able to*)

___

6. You helped me. (*to be supposed to*)

 ____

7. The children are careful. (*ought to*)

 ____

8. Why do they live in that little apartment? (*should*)

 ____

9. I have often traveled to Europe. (*to want to*)

 ____

10. Nick reads all the books on the top shelf. (*may*)

 ____

11. We will take the train as far as Chicago. (*to have to*)

 ____

12. They spoke with very little accent. (*to be able to*)

 ____

13. Do you help the child tie his shoes? (*can*)

 ____

14. The designers turn their work in on time. (*to be supposed to*)

 ____

15. Will Victor work overtime tomorrow? (*to have to*)

 ____

Exercise 1.8 Remove the auxiliaries from the following sentences and rewrite them appropriately. Maintain the same tense as in the original sentence.

1. We don't want to go to the movies.

____

2. He shouldn't eat so fast.

____

3. After supper we needed to take a little nap.

____

4. Tomorrow I'll have to go shopping for a new hat.

____

5. Why must you always lie to me?

____

6. Theresa hasn't been able to help her grandmother this week.

____

7. The guests may leave their coats at the door.

____

8. Vera was supposed to get everyone a little gift.

____

9. If you need to contact me after nine o'clock, call this number.

____

10. At what time should we go for lunch?

____

11. The tourists wanted to go to the museum early.

____

12. Juanita has to go out on a date with Richard.

____

13. This ought to be enough.

____

14. I have wanted to see the Grand Canyon.

____

15. My nephew hadn't been able to repair his car yet.

____

Exercise 1.9 Fill in the blanks in the following sentences with any appropriate auxiliary of your choosing.

1. We ________________ go to the opera.
2. Roberto ________________ play soccer with a neighborhood team.
3. Why ________________ it rain every Saturday?
4. During the summer her family always ________________ go swimming.
5. The new employees ________________ fill out some applications.
6. You ________________ be quiet in a library.

7. My aunt ________________ not spend so much money.

8. The boy never ________________ deliver the newspaper on time.

9. The old man ________________ walk very carefully.

10. These men and women ________________ learn several languages.

11. His apartment ________________ be on the third floor.

12. ________________ I help you?

13. When ________________ we finally see the new baby?

14. There ________________ be a better way to do this.

15. Joe always ________________ learn to play the guitar.

Exercise 1.10 Complete each sentence that follows with any appropriate phrase.

1. Do you always have to ________________________________?

2. When can she ________________________________?

3. Her mother hasn't been able ________________________________.

4. Tomorrow I need to ________________________________.

5. Should Raquel ________________________________?

6. After work we were supposed ________________________________.

7. Her boyfriend ought ________________________________.

8. My parents have always wanted to ________________________________.

9. Next week I'll need to ________________________________.

10. May I ________________________________?

11. Tom shouldn't ______________________________.

12. Yesterday I wasn't able to ______________________________.

13. I've often needed to ______________________________.

14. The new foreman just couldn't ______________________________.

15. Why must you ______________________________?

The Passive Voice

This verb structure is formed by the conjugation of the verb *to be* followed by the past participle of a transitive verb (a verb that can take a direct object). The following examples will be given in the third person singular.

	TO BE FOUND	**TO BE COOKED**
Present	is found	is cooked
Past	was found	was cooked
Present Perfect	has been found	has been cooked
Past Perfect	had been found	had been cooked
Future	will be found	will be cooked
Future Perfect	will have been found	will have been cooked

The passive is often used when you do not know who the person was that carried out a certain action. In the active voice, the subject (or the person who carries out a certain action) is obvious: "*A strange man* stole her purse." In the passive sentence, the direct object (her purse) becomes the new subject, and the verb (stole) is changed to the past participle (stolen). You can say in the passive voice, "Her purse was stolen by a strange man." If you don't know who the thief is, you can say, "Her purse was stolen."

Exercise 1.11 Rewrite the following sentences in the tenses shown. Notice that these sentences contain the passive voice structure (*to be* plus past participles).

1. Present ______________________________
   Past *Was the window repaired?*
   Present Perfect ______________________________

Past Perfect ____
Future ____
Future Perfect ____

2. Present ____
Past *The dog was struck by a car.* ____
Present Perfect ____
Past Perfect ____
Future ____
Future Perfect ____

3. Present ____
Past ____
Present Perfect *The package has been shipped by rail.* ____
Past Perfect ____
Future ____
Future Perfect ____

4. Present ____
Past ____
Present Perfect *Everything has been arranged.* ____
Past Perfect ____
Future ____
Future Perfect ____

5. Present ____
Past ____
Present Perfect ____
Past Perfect *The fort had been attacked at dawn.* ____
Future ____
Future Perfect ____

6. Present ____
Past ____
Present Perfect ____
Past Perfect *Her driver's license had been taken away.* ____
Future ____
Future Perfect ____

7. Present __________
   Past __________
   Present Perfect __________
   Past Perfect __________
   Future *A new song will be written for the rock concert.*
   Future Perfect __________

8. Present __________
   Past __________
   Present Perfect __________
   Past Perfect __________
   Future *Will the injured man be rescued in time?*
   Future Perfect __________

9. Present __________
   Past __________
   Present Perfect __________
   Past Perfect __________
   Future __________
   Future Perfect *Won't the damage have been noticed by then?*

10. Present *The king is whisked away to safety.*
    Past __________
    Present Perfect __________
    Past Perfect __________
    Future __________
    Future Perfect __________

Exercise 1.12 Some part of the passive structure is missing in each sentence. Fill in the blank with the appropriate form of the verb given in parentheses ( ). For example: "He *has* been given a prize." (*to have*)

1. The cadets are __________ marched toward the barracks. (*to be*)

2. Our country had never been __________ before. (*to attack*)

3. Yesterday he __________ sent to New York on business. (*to be*)

4. Had the house ________________ destroyed, too? (*to be*)

5. I can't ________________ bothered with such nonsense. (*to be*)

6. The baby was ________________ by his young mother. (*to change*)

7. Not a word had been ________________ in the dying man's room. (*to speak*)

8. His story ________________ believed, and he was sent to prison. (*not to be*)

9. The old barn was ________________ down by the storm. (*to blow*)

10. What has ________________ done to improve the situation? (*to be*)

11. The old woman ________________ been seen for days. (*to have not*)

12. War was ________________ in December of 1941. (*to declare*)

13. Your case will ________________ taken under consideration tomorrow. (*to be*)

14. The team was ________________ coached by a newcomer. (*to be*)

15. The pup ________________ being trained to stay in the kitchen. (*to be*)

The Subjunctive Mode

The subjunctive mode has a limited use in English. But to write well, you should have an understanding of it.

The present subjunctive is used when you give a *recommendation*, *suggestion*, or *command*. Let's look at some examples:

Tom suggested the boys *be* on time tomorrow. (not *are*)
The king commanded that the army *go* to the front immediately. (not *goes*)
We suggest Maria *have* a good night's sleep. (not *has*)
I recommend she *visit* the doctor as soon as possible. (not *visits*)

Present subjunctive conjugations are quite simple. The present subjunctive is formed from the infinitive and has no endings. Compare the present subjunctive of *to be*, *to have*, and *to go* with the present indicative (the form of the verb you already know).

INDICATIVE	SUBJUNCTIVE	INDICATIVE	SUBJUNCTIVE	INDICATIVE	SUBJUNCTIVE
I am	be	have	have	go	go
you are	be	have	have	go	go
he is	be	has	have	goes	go
we are	be	have	have	go	go
they are	be	have	have	go	go

Use the past subjunctive conjugation when you want to express a *wish*. The phrase often begins with *if*:

If only Juan *were* here.
If I just *had* another twenty dollars.

The past subjunctive is also used to set up a present condition (*If this were the case, that would happen*). The phrase beginning with *if* sets the condition.

If it *stopped* raining, I *would be* very happy.
If you *understood* my problem, you *would offer* me better advice.
I *wouldn't do* that if I *were* you.

Notice that *would* and a verb are used in the phrase that does not contain *if*.

The past subjunctive is formed from the simple past tense and, except for the verb *to be*, looks just like the past tense. Look at some examples with the verbs *to be*, *to have*, and *to look*.

INDICATIVE	SUBJUNCTIVE	INDICATIVE	SUBJUNCTIVE	INDICATIVE	SUBJUNCTIVE
I was	were	had	had	looked	looked
you were	were	had	had	looked	looked
he was	were	had	had	looked	looked
we were	were	had	had	looked	looked
they were	were	had	had	looked	looked

In certain cases, the verb can be preceded by *would*. This use will be explained later. The preceding three verbs become *would be*, *would have*, and *would look*.

When you use a verb with an auxiliary (is going, has spoken, is able to write), the same pattern occurs as shown previously. In the phrase that begins with *if*, use the auxiliary and participle. In the other phrase, use *would* followed by the auxiliary and participle. The phrase that begins with *if* sets the *past condition*. Let's look at some examples:

If he *had earned* enough money, he *would have been going* to college next fall.
Tom *would have spoken* with you if he *had seen* you.
If you *had studied* harder, you *would have been able to write* better.

Exercise 1.13 Fill in the blank with the correct form of the verb shown.

1. I have to recommend you ________________ (*to speak*) with her soon.

2. The sultan commanded she ________________ (*to sing*) for him.

3. Maria suggested he ________________ (*to find*) someone else to dance with.

4. The boss recommended they ________________ (*to be*) on time from now on.

5. If only he ________________ (*to have*) not drunk so much.

6. I ________________ (*to be*) so happy if she came for a visit.

7. If you ________________ (*to play*) harder, we ________________ (*to win*) the game.

8. Juan ________________ (*have bought*) the car if it ________________ (*have been*) cheaper.

9. If only mother ________________ (*to be*) well again.

10. The lawyer suggested the man ________________ (*to hire*) someone else.

11. If the girl ________________ (*have seen*) the accident, she ________________ (*have reported*) it immediately.

12. Long ________________ (*to live*) the king!

13. Tom ________________ (*to speak*) with her if she ________________ (*to smile*) at him.

14. I ________________ (*have helped*) you if I ________________ (*have known*) how ill you are.

15. She suggested the man ________________ (*to be*) prepared for a blood test.

Exercise 1.14 Change the verbs in the following sentences from a *present condition* to a *past condition* by adding the auxiliary *have* and changing the verb to a past participle. For example: "If he came along, I would be glad." When you add *have* it changes to: "If he had come along, I would have been glad."

1. If Jorge were at home, he would answer the telephone.

   ____

2. If you earned enough money, you would be able to buy the car.

   ____

3. If Alicia sent him a picture, he would be the happiest man alive.

   ____

4. I wouldn't say such a thing if I were the boss.

   ____

5. My brother would sell the old radio if it were his.

   ____

6. Would you really kiss me if I asked you to?

   ____

7. If Mr. Johnson got a ticket, his wife would be very angry with him.

____

8. If it snowed, they would have to go skiing.

____

9. If Robert overslept again, he would lose his job.

____

10. If only my sister were here.

____

11. Would you trust me again if I gave you my word of honor?

____

12. I wouldn't like it at all if Barbara went out with Bill.

____

13. If the carpenter had time, he would build you a nice cabinet.

____

14. If he knew the truth, he wouldn't write such a nasty letter.

____

15. If Enrique worked harder, he wouldn't need to work overtime.

____

Exercise 1.15 Now change the following sentences from a *past condition* to a *present condition*. For example: "If he had come along, I would have been glad." When you remove the auxiliary, it changes to: "If he came along, I would be glad."

1. If only he had seen the truck in time.

 ____

2. I wouldn't have given her the money if I had known why she wanted it.

 ____

3. Would you have cared if I had gone out on a date with Carmen?

 ____

4. Maria would have had to stay overnight if she had missed the last train.

 ____

5. If I hadn't had a flat tire, I wouldn't have missed the sale.

 ____

6. If only you had been able to forgive me.

 ____

7. The boss would have fired her if he had seen her sleeping on the job.

 ____

8. If he had needed to borrow some money, he would have come to me.

 ____

9. The thief would have been caught if the police had arrived sooner.

____

10. If the computer had been repaired, the data files would have been finished on time.

____

Exercise 1.16 Complete the following sentences with any appropriate phrase.

1. If Juanita had seen me at the store, ____________________.

2. If you were my friend, ____________________.

3. If only the money ____________________ today.

4. I would be so grateful if ____________________.

5. Tom wouldn't have left you there if ____________________.

6. Would you help the old woman if ____________________?

7. If ____________________, the kitchen would be painted by now.

8. If ____________________, we would have arranged a party for her.

9. If you had earned a few dollars more, ____________________.

10. Wouldn't it be a wonderful surprise if ____________________?

Conjunctions

In this part you will be dealing with conjunctions. They are used to combine two sentences into one—a compound sentence. Some conjunctions have an adverbial usage, but here you will encounter them as they are used in everyday language: as words that combine two phrases or sentences into one.

If the combined sentences each have a subject and a verb, separate the sentences with a comma:

John is a doctor, and Mary is a lawyer.
John is a doctor and works in Chicago.

If the combined sentences begin with a conjunction, separate them with a comma:

If you work hard, you can have a good life.

When using *however* or *therefore*, you should separate the combined sentences with a semicolon:

His hands were tied; however, he continued to struggle to get free.
There's a storm coming; therefore we have to stay alert.

The use of the comma is optional when the two parts of the sentence are related or are linked by meaning:

Alicia is smart, but she hates to study.
Alicia is smart but she hates to study.

Following are some commonly used conjunctions:

and
because
but
for
however
if
since
therefore

Look at the following examples:

There was nothing the doctor could do; *therefore* he left.
Anna is a smart girl, *but* she just doesn't like studying.
Because she became ill, Maria couldn't go to the party.

Interrogative pronouns, which ask a question, can also be used as conjunctions. They are not true conjunctions, but they can still be used to combine two sentences into one. These are interrogative pronouns:

how
what
when
where
why

Look at these examples:

I don't know *why* you have to go so early.
Can you tell me *how* I can find Green Street?
When John came into the room, she began to blush.

Exercise 1.17 Choose the appropriate conjunction from the two given, and rewrite the two sentences as one.

1. We went to bed early. (*if, because*) It was such a tiring day.

____

2. Can you tell me? (*and, where*) John is working.

____

3. Monday is the first day of classes. (*and, why*) I still have to buy some books.

____

4. Juan is my only brother. (*therefore, but*) I haven't seen him in a year.

____

5. The weather is terrible today. (*however, when*) The parade went on as planned.

____

6. She started crying. (*if, when*) I told her I love her.

___

7. I don't understand. (*since, how*) You can live in the city.

___

8. The soldiers let out a cheer. (*for, where*) The war had finally ended.

___

9. Tom will help you. (*if, since*) You pay him a few dollars.

___

10. We didn't know. (*therefore, where*) She was hiding.

___

11. Let me know. (*however, when*) You will be home.

___

12. It's been a long time. (*since, if*) I last saw you.

___

13. Do your very best. (*if, but*) Be careful.

___

14. She suddenly understood. (*where, but*) Father got the money.

___

15. It's difficult to understand. (*why, what*) We should help you.

___

Exercise 1.18 Complete the following sentences with any appropriate phrase.

1. The children remained in the garden and ______________________.
2. In summer it's terribly hot, but ______________________.
3. Juan hates mathematics because ______________________.
4. Helena decided to stay home, for ______________________.
5. They all stayed inside their tents because ______________________.
6. We have no more money; therefore ______________________.
7. I'm very disappointed; however, ______________________.
8. Martin will lend us some money if ______________________.
9. Do you know why ______________________?
10. I think I can tell you what ______________________.
11. I wonder how ______________________.
12. The policeman asked me when ______________________.
13. When ______________________, I suddenly felt afraid.
14. The ancient map showed where ______________________.
15. If ______________________, Professor Smith will cancel the exam.
16. I know you're telling the truth, but ______________________.
17. The storm is over, and ______________________.
18. I knew we were in trouble when ______________________.

19. You'll get a big raise in pay if ______________________________.

20. I just want to know when ______________________________.

Exercise 1.19 Complete the following sentences with any appropriate phrase.

1. ______________________________, and I quickly ran away.

2. ______________________________, but the bird died anyway.

3. ______________________________ because he lost his key.

4. ______________________________, for it was raining cats and dogs.

5. ______________________________, because Isabel had bought the tickets.

6. ______________________________; therefore they just stayed at work.

7. ______________________________; however, I prefer classical music.

8. If the carpenters earn enough money, ______________________________.

9. ______________________________ why Charles should go along.

10. ______________________________ what made you lie to me.

11. ______________________________ how a computer works.

12. ______________________________ who robbed the bank.

13. When I drove up to the grocery store, ______________________________.

14. ______________________________ when Mother saw the package on the table.

15. ______________________________ where you bought the ring.

Pronouns

A pronoun is a word that can replace a noun in a sentence. English has four basic pronouns that can replace a noun. A noun referring to males (man, boy, gentleman) is replaced by *he*. A noun referring to females (girl, mother, lady) is replaced by *she*. A noun referring to an inanimate object (house, rock, window) is replaced by *it*. And all plural nouns (boys, children, rocks) are replaced by *they*. The pronoun *we* is the replacement for *a noun plus I*: Tom and I = we, the girls and I = we.

But the pronouns just given (he, she, it, they, we) are used only as the subject of a sentence. Pronouns have other forms, which are used as objects or possessives.

SUBJECT	OBJECT	POSSESSIVE	INDEPENDENT POSSESSIVE
he	him	his	his
she	her	her	hers
it	it	its	its
they	them	their	theirs
we	us	our	ours

An independent possessive pronoun is one that replaces a possessive pronoun and a noun. It is independent. It can stand alone.

This one is *his book*. = This one is *his*.
Her dress is rather dirty. = *Hers* is rather dirty.
Its right fender has a dent. = *Its* has a dent.
Where is *their tent*? = Where is *theirs*?
Our brother works in Chicago. = *Ours* works in Chicago.

Although the pronouns *I* and *you* do not replace nouns, they follow the same pattern as the pronouns already shown.

SUBJECT	OBJECT	POSSESSIVE	INDEPENDENT POSSESSIVE
I	me	my	mine
you	you	your	yours

Exercise 1.20 Replace the italicized noun or noun phrase in the following sentences with the appropriate pronoun. Be careful: not all of the italicized nouns are subjects.

1. *The lawyer* stood up slowly and looked at the jury.

 ____

2. When I saw *the girls* on the corner, I gave a little wave.

 ____

3. I knew that *the tall woman* was our new boss.

 ____

4. Dr. Brown often wrote about *that operation* in her diary.

 ____

5. *Their problems* were really much worse than mine.

 ____

6. I truly liked *Mr. Johnson's* daughter a lot.

 ____

7. *Robert and I* hoped to buy a car together.

 ____

8. I'd help if *Alicia's* brother would help.

 ____

9. I think that the last two chairs at the table are *our chairs.*

____

10. You ought to have a few words with *that rude man.*

____

Exercise 1.21 Change the italicized possessive noun or noun phrase to the appropriate pronoun.

1. *The children's* bedroom needs to be painted.

____

2. Have you met *Tom's* relatives?

____

3. It looks like *the car's* trunk is scratched.

____

4. Why is *the magazine's* cover torn off?

____

5. Her aunt is a physician in one of *the city's* clinics.

____

6. *Her uncle's* neighbor used to work as a gardener.

____

7. *The actress'* voice began to crack.

____

8. Was *your sister's* husband a carpenter, too?

____

9. *Their new apartment* is really too small for their family.

____

10. I'd like to see *your friends'* new house sometime.

____

Reflexive Pronouns

A reflexive pronoun is easily identified by the ending *-self* for a singular (myself, yourself, himself, herself, itself) and *-selves* for a plural (ourselves, yourselves, themselves). It is the object acted upon by a pronoun subject of the same form. Look at the following table:

SUBJECT PRONOUN	OBJECT PRONOUN	REFLEXIVE PRONOUN
I	me	myself
you (singular)	you	yourself
he	him	himself
she	her	herself
it	it	itself
we	us	ourselves
you (plural)	you	yourselves
they	them	themselves

If the subject acts upon an object that is a different pronoun, use an object pronoun. If the subject and object are the same pronoun, use a reflexive pronoun. Look at these examples:

I protect you. I protect him. I protect them. I protect *myself.*
He helps me. He helps her. He helps us. He helps *himself.*
We ask you. We ask him. We ask them. We ask *ourselves.*
They talk to me. They talk to you. They talk to her. They talk to *themselves.*

Exercise 1.22 Fill in the blank with the appropriate form of the pronoun shown in parentheses ( ).

1. We usually bathe ________________ in the river. (*we*)
2. I can't understand ________________. (*he*)
3. I've always told ________________ to be careful. (*I*)
4. My girlfriend wants to buy ________________ a new skirt. (*she*)
5. Did you get these magazines from ________________? (*they*)
6. The new boss prides ________________ on being fair. (*he*)
7. You both seemed to enjoy ________________ at the party. (*you*)
8. The magician's rope rose up from the ground by ________________. (*it*)
9. The animals try to protect ________________ from the wind. (*they*)
10. The guard couldn't protect ________________ from an attack. (*they*)
11. I sent ________________ several postcards from Mexico. (*she*)
12. Carlos raised the camera and took a picture of ________________. (*he*)
13. I'm not afraid of ________________ at all. (*it*)
14. Tom, you should be ashamed of ________________. (*you*)
15. Raquel and I are proud of ________________ for what we did. (*we*)

Exercise 1.23 Use the pronouns listed in the following and write three short sentences: (a) use the pronoun as a subject, (b) use the pronoun as a direct object or the object of a preposition, and (c) use the pronoun as a possessive.

Example: He

a. He is my friend. (subject)
b. I visit him often. (direct object) This is for him. (object of preposition)
c. His father is a butcher. (possessive)

1. I
 a. ______
 b. ______
 c. ______

2. You
 a. ______
 b. ______
 c. ______

3. She
 a. ______
 b. ______
 c. ______

4. We
 a. ______
 b. ______
 c. ______

5. They
 a. ______
 b. ______
 c. ______

6. It
 a. ______
 b. ______
 c. ______

7. He
 a. ______
 b. ______
 c. ______

Relative Pronouns

A relative pronoun is a word that does two things: (1) It replaces a noun or pronoun in the sentence. (2) It combines the sentence with a second sentence. Look at the two sentences that follow. The phrase *the officer* is in both sentences:

> *The officer* saw him speeding. *The officer* gave him a ticket.

These two sentences can be combined by changing one of the phrases *the officer* to a relative pronoun. The English relative pronouns are *who* or *that* for people and *which* or *that* for things. See how the preceding sentences are changed:

> The officer, who saw him speeding, gave him a ticket.
>
> **or**
>
> The officer, who gave him a ticket, saw him speeding.

It is generally a good rule to use a comma before *who* or *which* in a relative clause. This is especially true when that clause simply provides additional information about the antecedent. If the clause specifies "which person" or "which thing," the comma should be omitted. The relative pronoun *that* can also be used.

> The officer that saw him speeding gave him a ticket.
>
> **or**
>
> The officer that gave him a ticket saw him speeding.

Notice that there is a tendency to avoid commas with *that*. Look at a few more examples:

> I like *the girl. The girl* lives down that street.
> I like the girl who lives down that street.
>
> **or**
>
> I like the girl that lives down that street.

He said *a word*. I don't understand *a word*.
He said a word, which I don't understand.

or

He said a word that I don't understand.

Where's *the car*? You bought *the car*.
Where's the car that you bought?

or

Where's the car you bought?

Let's take a closer look at relative pronouns and the clauses they form. English forms relative clauses in four ways:

1. With the relative pronoun *who* or *whom*, when referring to people. *Who* is used as the subject of a sentence. *Whom* is used in all other cases. *Whose* replaces a possessive adjective (my, his, our, et cetera).
2. With the relative pronoun *that* when referring to people or things.
3. With the relative pronoun *which* when referring to things.
4. By omitting the relative pronoun when it is a *direct object* or the *object of a preposition*. This is called an *elliptical* relative pronoun. (You encountered this in one of the earlier examples: "Where's the car you bought?")

Study the following examples:

1. That's the man *who* stole my briefcase. (subject of the clause)
   That's the man *whom* we met in Boston. (direct object)
   That's the man *whose* son is a professional soccer player. (possessive: *his son*)

2. Who's the student *that* wrote this paper? (person)
   I found the ball *that* was kicked over the fence. (thing)

3. I found the ball, *which* was kicked over the fence. (thing)

4. That's the man we met in Boston. (elliptical: *whom* is omitted)
   This is the boy I bought the toy for. (elliptical: *whom* is omitted and the preposition *for* is placed at the end of the sentence)

Note: in casual language *whom* is nearly always replaced by *who*.

You need to be careful when using prepositions with relative pronouns. Their position in a sentence can vary. Look at the following examples, and study how the preposition can be placed.

They bought the house. An old man died in the house.
They bought the house in which an old man died.
They bought the house which an old man died in.
They bought the house that an old man died in.
They bought the house an old man died in.

I visited the man. I got a gift from the man.
I visited the man, from whom I got a gift.
I visited the man who(m) I got a gift from.
I visited the man that I got a gift from.
I visited the man I got a gift from.

Exercise 1.24 Combine the following pairs of sentences by using a relative pronoun.

1. We decided to buy the newspaper. The newspaper was printed in London.

   ____

2. Helena caught a fish. The fish was nearly two feet long.

   ____

3. Are you going to rent the apartment? William lived in the apartment.

   ____

4. I have often chatted with the policeman. My father knows the policeman.

 ____

5. There was a horrible storm. The storm destroyed many trees.

 ____

6. We're going to the beach. My grandparents live near the beach.

 ____

7. May I have the bike? The bike is in need of repair.

 ____

8. They all like the new boss. The new boss got them pay raises.

 ____

9. David's mother is in the hospital. The hospital is located on Main Street.

 ____

10. Do you have the money? I put the money on this table.

 ____

11. The children were lost in the forest. An ugly witch lived in the forest.

 ____

12. I don't understand the problem. You wrote about the problem in your letter.

 ____

13. Several men found the bear. The bear's cubs had died.

____

14. She shouldn't wear the dress. The dress has a stain on it.

____

15. They captured the officer. The officer's troops attacked the fort.

____

Exercise 1.25 Restate each relative clause that follows as an *elliptical* relative clause.

This is the coat that I found. = *This is the coat I found.*

1. She agreed to buy the car that I saw in the city.

____

2. Do you have the money that I lent you?

____

3. Where's the lamp that I put on this table?

____

4. That's the fellow that I got the tickets from.

____

5. Tom got a job in the factory in which my father works.

____

6. Where did you find the books which I lost?

____

7. Juan wrote the poem that Maria is reading right now.

____

8. Help me find the kitten that the dog chased into the garden.

____

9. There's the airline pilot whom we visited last week.

____

10. The thief stole the camera which I had placed on this bench a moment ago.

____

11. This is the heroic boy that the reporter wrote about.

____

12. I was the one who bought the bottle of beer that Robert drank.

____

13. Our boss fired the girl with whom he had argued.

____

14. Carmen lived in the same town that I lived in years ago.

____

15. Why did you break the window which Dad just repaired?

____

Exercise 1.26 Complete the following sentences with any appropriate relative clause. You should use the relative pronoun given. Omit the relative pronoun where indicated.

1. We spent several days in the valley, which ________________.
2. I like the story from which ________________.
3. Do you know the fellow who ________________?
4. Father met a rich man whom ________________.
5. I like the novels (*omit*) ________________.
6. The trucks head up the mountain that ________________.
7. Have you seen the movie (*omit*) ________________?
8. I still need to buy a computer that ________________.
9. We all enjoy the hilarious comedian whose ________________.
10. Ask the cashier from whom ________________.
11. We're going to the new restaurant (*omit*) ________________.
12. Charles bought a CD player that ________________.
13. We're driving to the mountains (*omit*) ________________.
14. They have a serious problem, which ________________.
15. She'll never forget the present (*omit*) ________________.

Possessive Relative Pronouns

There are two forms of possessive for relative pronouns. One refers to people or other living things: *whose*. The other is a prepositional phrase using *of*.

When you combine two sentences with a relative pronoun, and the noun you change to a relative pronoun is possessive (the boy's, a writer's), use *whose* as the relative pronoun. Look at these examples:

I saw the man. *The man's* house had burned down.
I saw the man *whose* house had burned down.

I like the girl. *The girl's* new car is a red convertible.
I like the girl *whose* new car is a red convertible.

But when the possessive noun is an inanimate object, use a prepositional phrase with *of*. Look at these examples:

I found a book. *The book's* cover was torn and dirty.
I found a book, the cover *of which* was torn and dirty.

You'll recognize their house. The color *of their house* is bright yellow.
You'll recognize their house, the color *of which* is bright yellow.

I have some lumber. The length *of the lumber* is perfect for this project.
I have some lumber, the length *of which* is perfect for this project.

No matter how the inanimate object forms its possessive (the book's or of the book), the relative pronoun is formed as a prepositional phrase (of which).

Exercise 1.27 Combine the following sentences. Use the appropriate possessive form of the relative pronoun.

1. I helped the young student. The young student's grades were terrible.

 ____

2. Where's the fellow? The fellow's car won't start.

 ____

3. I bought an old car. The interior of the old car was in bad condition.

 ____

4. Where's the woman? The woman's husband still lives in Mexico.

____

5. I need a carton. The carton's size has to be two feet by three feet by three feet.

____

6. Juan discovered a cave. The cave's ceiling was more than thirty feet high.

____

7. The doctor examined the child. The child's temperature was over one hundred degrees.

____

8. The teacher punished the boys. The boys' behavior was awful.

____

9. He reread the words. The meaning of the words was beyond his understanding.

____

10. Juanita tasted the cake. The cake's flavor was wonderful.

____

Possessives and Plurals

English possessives of nouns are usually formed in two ways: (1) by placing *of* before a noun or (2) by adding *-'s* to the noun. The preposition *of* tends to be used with inanimate objects, and *-'s* tends to be used with people or living things. But often either one can be used. Look at these examples:

the color of the car, the car's color
the depth of the river, the river's depth
the face of a man, a man's face
the roar of the lion, the lion's roar

The ending *-'s* is used for most singular nouns. But if a singular noun already ends in *-s*, just add an apostrophe to make it possessive (Mr. Jones' car, Chris' house). However, an apostrophe with an *-s* can also be used (Mr. Jones's car, Chris's house). Some examples of words that can take either form of the possessive follow.

SINGULAR NOUN	POSSESSIVE -'	POSSESSIVE -'S
boss	boss'	boss's
class	class'	class's
gas	gas'	gas's
miss	miss'	miss's

Most plural nouns already end in *-s*. In that case, just add an apostrophe (two boys' bikes, those girls' books). But some plural nouns are irregular. These form their possessive by adding *-'s*, but the meaning is still plural.

one goose	two geese	two geese's eggs
one man	two men	two men's suits
one woman	five women	five women's shoes
one mouse	ten mice	ten mice's babies

Plurals are formed very simply in English: add *-s* or *-es* to most words. If a word ends in *-s*, *-z*, *-sh*, *-x*, or *-ch*, add *-es* for the plural. When a word ends in *-y*, it tends to form the plural by changing *-y* to *-i* and adding *-es* (candy, candies; lady, ladies; penny, pennies). There are some exceptions to that rule, for example, when *-y* follows a vowel (buy, buys; key, keys; joy, joys). In all other cases, form the plural with *-s*. Some examples:

bus, buses
buzz, buzzes
wash, washes
box, boxes
perch, perches
baby, babies
laundry, laundries

country, countries
try, tries
job, jobs
kid, kids
song, songs
ladder, ladders
shipment, shipments

The list of irregular plurals is quite short: child, children; foot, feet; goose, geese; man, men; mouse, mice; ox, oxen; person, people; tooth, teeth; woman, women.

Here's a simple rule for knowing whether a word is used as a plural or a possessive: plurals end in *-s*. Possessives end in *-'s* or *-s'*.

Look what happens to definite (the) and indefinite (a, an) articles when a noun changes from singular to plural:

the boy, the boys
the clock, the clocks
a river, rivers
an apple, apples

The indefinite article in the plural is dropped, and the plural word stands alone. The difference between the definite and indefinite article usage is the same for both the singular and plural. The definite article is specific—a certain person or thing that you are thinking about (the man, the car, the problems). The indefinite article defines a word as unspecific—it is *any* person or thing (a man, a car, problems).

Exercise 1.28 In the following, change the italicized words to the correct form of possessive.

1. *The young man* ____________________ friend was very sick.

2. The dark brown ____________________ *her eyes* was beautiful.

3. I hope *the jury* ____________________ verdict is fair.

4. They couldn't hear *the captain* ____________________ commands.

5. *The women* ____________________ calls for help went unheard.

6. She didn't understand the meaning ________________ *his words.*

7. *Our teams* ________________ records were really poor.

8. This year *our team* ________________ playing was much improved.

9. The economy ________________ *these countries* is growing.

10. *Thomas* ________________ father is a carpenter.

Exercise 1.29 Rewrite the sentences and change all italicized nouns to the plural. Don't forget to change verbs and other words wherever necessary.

1. The *goose* had laid a golden *egg.*

____

2. My *uncle* bought the *house* at the edge of town.

____

3. The *church* was damaged by the *storm.*

____

4. A *soldier* carried the helpless *infant* to safety.

____

5. Did the *woman* find her *child*?

____

6. A strange *man* came up to the *window* and looked in.

____

7. Their *boss* is going to fire the new *employee.*

____

8. A large *board* fell on Juan and broke his *foot*.

____

9. The *city* is too far from the *factory*.

____

10. The *nurse* covered the *patient* with a heavy *blanket*.

____

Exercise 1.30 Look at the phrases in parentheses ( ). Decide which phrase best completes each sentence.

1. (*The boys, The boy's, The boys'*) The girls have tents on the other side of the lake. ________________ tents are here.

2. (*the animals, the animal's*) I looked at ________________ in such small cages and felt sad.

3. (*your parents, your parents'*) Is this ________________ new house?

4. (*the man, the men, the men's*) Can you tell me where ________________ room is?

5. (*Mr. Roberts, Mr. Roberts'*) ________________ daughter now lives in Seattle.

6. (*of names, of names'*) I found the list ________________ in the desk drawer.

7. (*the airports, the airport's*) Why are ________________ located so far from town?

8. (*a grown woman, grown women, the grown women's*) It's true that ________________ has a lot of responsibilities.

9. (*soups, of soup, the soup's*) A large bowl ________________ costs two dollars.

10. (*eggs, the egg's, the eggs'*) The cook needs a dozen ________________.

11. (*the bosses, the boss'*) Someone parked in ________________ parking space.

12. (*The tourist, The tourists, The tourist's*) ________________ visa seemed to be in order.

13. (*my sisters, my brother's, of my cousins*) That's ________________ new car on the corner.

14. (*his stories, his story's, his stories'*) I always enjoyed ________________ as a child.

15. (*Tom's foot, Tom's feet, Tom's feet's*) ________________ are swollen and red.

The Comparative and Superlative

The ordinary form of an adjective or adverb is called the *positive*. Some examples: tall, rich, interesting, quickly, slowly, magically.

But you will want to use the *comparative* of an adjective or adverb to show a contrast between two people or things. The word *than* separates the two contrasting ideas.

The comparative is formed by adding *-er* to most adjectives or adverbs. If the adjective ends in *-y*, change the *-y* to *-i*. Then add *-er*. Let's look at a few examples:

tall = John is *taller than* Juanita.
brave = The captain acted *braver than* any other soldier.
funny = I thought this book was *funnier than* that one.

For longer words, comparatives are usually formed by adding the word *more* before the adjective or adverb, as in the following:

intelligent = Mike is really *more intelligent than* Tom.
interesting = Your last article was *more interesting than* the one you wrote in June.
fluently = Juan speaks *more fluently than* his father.

The *superlative* form describes the greatest or least quality of a person or thing. It is usually formed by adding *-est* to an adjective or adverb and usually by placing *the* in front of it. If the adjective ends in *-y*, change *-y* to *-i*. Then add *-est*. Let's look at some examples:

tall = My father's *the tallest* man in the family.
brave = The wounded man fought *the bravest* of them all.
funny = He knows *the funniest* stories.

For longer words, superlatives are usually formed by adding the words *the most* before the adjective or adverb, as in the following:

intelligent = I think my grandfather is *the most intelligent*.
interesting = *The most interesting* thing about the movie was the music.
fluently = She speaks *the most fluently* of anyone I know.

English has a few irregular forms in the comparative and superlative that just have to be memorized:

POSITIVE	COMPARATIVE	SUPERLATIVE
good	better	(the) best
well	better	(the) best
bad	worse	(the) worst
much (singular)	more	(the) most
many (plural)	more	(the) most
little (amount)	less	(the) least

Exercise 1.31 Change the italicized adjective or adverb to the comparative. Use the word in parentheses ( ) to make the contrast. For example, you will see: "Michael is *tall*. (*Bill*)" You should write: "Michael is taller than Bill."

1. My sister is *pretty*. (*my cousin*)

____

2. Our team played *poorly*. (*your team*)

____

3. Uncle William was *rich*. (*Uncle James*)

____

4. Raquel can run *fast*. (*her brother*)

____

5. The roses are *delicate*. (*the daisies*)

____

6. Thomas really works *well*. (*anyone else*)

____

7. Finding a job is *important*. (*watching TV*)

____

8. He wrote his signature *rapidly*. (*the address*)

____

9. Ms. Johnson is *friendly*. (*Mr. Johnson*)

____

10. Can you speak *loudly*? (*James*)

____

11. Tom is *responsible*. (*his sister*)

____

12. A fox is *sly*. (*a rabbit*)

____

13. My nephew knows *many* funny stories. (*my niece*)

____

14. The bees are *busy*. (*the ants*)

____

15. He knows *little* about math. *(history)*

____

Exercise 1.32 Change the italicized adjective or adverb to the superlative. For example, you will see: "Michael is *tall*." You should write: "Michael is the tallest."

1. My sister is *pretty*.

____

2. The *good* recipes are in this book.

____

3. Your nephew does *little* work around the house.

____

4. The *important* idea in the book is learning to be patient.

____

5. Maria swam *fast* and won a blue ribbon.

____

6. I have *many* problems.

____

7. I feel that Juan is the *intelligent* one.

____

8. Bill arrived *early* and left *late.*

____

9. The *old* car costs *little* money.

____

10. Your pronunciation is *bad.*

____

11. I think yours is a *good* idea.

____

12. An SUV is a *logical* choice for a family car.

____

13. My aunt has *much* money.

____

14. Alicia spoke *brilliantly* about the Civil War.

____

15. This brown puppy is *small.*

____

If you have completed all the exercises in this chapter with a high degree of accuracy, you are ready to go on to the next stage of the writing program. If you feel you need more review, repeat the exercises that gave you trouble.

2

Beginning to Write

Sentence Completion

In Chapter 1 you manipulated the sentences provided for you by changing the tense of the verb, changing the subject or object of the sentence, or adding words, such as auxiliaries and modifiers. And you dealt with these things separately in categories: verbs, pronouns, adjectives, passive voice, and so on. Upon completing that kind of practice, you are ready to write more creatively.

But before you begin to write original sentences, you should practice completing different kinds of sentences to test your skill with the things you practiced in Chapter 1. In this chapter's exercises you need to decide what word or phrase makes the most sense for completing each sentence. In each case you want to be sure that the *grammar* and the *meaning of the words* are appropriate.

A variety of elements are missing from the sentences in these exercises. Some require a subject, others a direct object or the object of a preposition. And still others are missing a verb or a modifier. Look at each sentence carefully, and decide what kind of element is missing and what meaning is required to make a good sentence.

Exercise 2.1 Write in the phrase that best completes each sentence.

1. It ______________________ to understand the problem.
   a. can't
   b. can't be able
   c. isn't difficult
   d. won't happen

2. I finally met the inventor, ______________________ changed how our company works.
   a. when he invented
   b. whose machine
   c. the idea of
   d. that concept

3. It was clever of ______________________ to disguise his voice.
    a. him
    b. thieves and robbers
    c. singing so quietly
    d. the moment

4. You mustn't ______________________ in an argument with her.
    a. back down
    b. to become angry
    c. forget
    d. have forgotten

5. Jack discovered ______________________ living under the porch.
    a. alive and well
    b. they had
    c. several tiny kittens
    d. never been

6. I would have left immediately ______________________ the storm hadn't been so bad.
    a. whether
    b. whether or not
    c. while
    d. if

7. ______________________ the summer months we like to stay in the north.
    a. During
    b. In spite
    c. As a result of
    d. Concerning

8. For some reason, the winner ______________________ than the loser.
    a. relied on him
    b. was more embarrassed
    c. received the most prizes
    d. lost

9. It's ______________________ that you'll ever find a job around here.
    a. rather doubtful
    b. surely
    c. up to you
    d. being a difficult situation

10. There are ______________________ I need to take up with you.
    a. several issues
    b. needless to say
    c. nevertheless
    d. apart from other problems

11. I suggest that Ms. Johnson ______________________ employment elsewhere.
    a. find
    b. seeks
    c. fills out an application
    d. wrote out an application

12. I don't see how this situation ______________________.
    a. will have to do
    b. can't be like that
    c. relates to me
    d. is concerning

13. I simply ______________________ for language like that.
    a. really care
    b. understand completely
    c. despise
    d. won't stand

14. I have no idea who ______________________ in the world is.
    a. came
    b. the richest man
    c. wanted to come
    d. a smart woman

15. Do you have any idea ______________________ this makes me feel?
    a. when
    b. in such a way
    c. of which
    d. how

16. Send me a memo ______________________ the new sales figures.
    a. regarding
    b. about it
    c. off
    d. when they are ready

17. The coat, ______________________ was terrible, was too short for her.
    a. she so often wears
    b. it
    c. of what
    d. the color of which

18. If you hadn't ______________________ there, things would have become much worse.
    a. been
    b. came
    c. had been
    d. have come

19. The reports aren't ready; ______________________ this meeting is concluded.
    a. or
    b. therefore
    c. in such a case
    d. resulting in

20. The soldiers couldn't find a way to protect ______________________.
    a. village
    b. from the villagers
    c. during the battle
    d. themselves

Exercise 2.2 You will see a variety of incomplete sentences, which you may complete in any appropriate way. Some are missing only one word. Others can be completed by adding a phrase. Study the examples that follow. Use them as your model as you go through the exercises.

> Mark *has* been my friend since kindergarten.
> She cried *when she fell on the ice*.
> I met a man *whose* son is also in college.

1. I ______________________ not help you today.
2. When ______________________, we decided to drive out into the country.
3. We'll be happy to join you at the party if ______________________.
4. My grandmother has ______________________ ill for two weeks.
5. Whenever I get too tired, I need ______________________ take a nap.
6. Next year the tourists ______________________ travel to Mexico.
7. I've been ______________________ about this problem all day.
8. Maria bought a dress, ______________________ only cost twenty dollars.
9. In weather like this you ______________________ wear a raincoat.
10. Everyone ______________________ to leave the park at ten o'clock.
11. Martin has to stay in bed ______________________ he broke his leg at the game last week.
12. The children have been ______________________ in the park for hours.
13. Mother ______________________ have finished the blouse by noon tomorrow.
14. You ______________________ come in, if you wish.

15. Mr. Brown ______________________ riding a beautiful white horse.

16. I need ______________________ borrow a few dollars from you.

17. He wasn't ______________________ to get the job done yesterday.

18. I found a wallet ______________________ probably belongs to you.

19. This is the woman ______________________ I work with.

20. I won't be going to work today because ______________________.

Exercise 2.3 You will see a variety of incomplete sentences, which you may complete in any appropriate way. Some are missing only one word. Others can be completed by adding a phrase.

1. ______________________ I'll have finished the repairs on your car.

2. ______________________ do they expect to land at the airport?

3. ______________________ is working in the laboratory now.

4. The valuable vase ______________________ broken sometime during the night.

5. The prisoners will be ______________________ to a different prison.

6. It is impossible to know ______________________________________.

7. I'm busy tomorrow; however, ___________________________________.

8. William suggested he ______________________________________.

9. I'm really not supposed ______________________________________.

10. Maria ______________________ be able to watch the children tonight.

11. The students ______________________ had time to prepare for the test.

12. My uncle ______________________, but my aunt ____________________.

13. They will have ______________ to the factory on their own.

14. I never ______________ because you never ______________.

15. If I understood ______________, I would ______________.

16. When I saw ______________, I knew you ______________.

17. He didn't ______________ because she didn't ______________.

18. Can you ______________ where the post office ______________?

19. I'm really sorry that ______________.

20. He finally met the beautiful actress that ______________.

21. My uncle sat next to ______________ I had been talking with.

22. If only my grandmother could ______________.

23. Do you know why ______________?

24. If I were you, I'd ______________.

25. I didn't ______________ because I knew ______________.

Exercise 2.4 You will see a variety of incomplete sentences, which you may complete in any appropriate way. Some are missing only one word. Others can be completed by adding a phrase.

1. ______________ because it was such a tiring day.

2. ______________ where John is working?

3. ______________, and I still have to find a job.

4. William is my only brother, but ______________.

5. ______________, but be very careful.

6. Maria loves rock concerts because ______________________________.

7. The twins decided to stay home, although ______________________.

8. They've been working at the mall since _________________________.

9. I don't have any money; therefore ______________________________.

10. She suddenly understood to whom ______________________________.

11. It's difficult to understand why _______________________________.

12. I know you're telling the truth, but ____________________________.

13. The storm is over, and ______________________________.

14. I knew we were in trouble when ______________________________.

15. The storm is over, but ______________________________.

16. You'll get a big raise in pay if ______________________________.

17. I just want to find out why ______________________________.

18. If you really were a good friend, ______________________________.

19. I wouldn't have said a word if ______________________________.

20. ______________________________ if you hadn't borrowed so much money.

Exercise 2.5 You will see a variety of incomplete sentences, which you may complete in any appropriate way. Some are missing only one word. Others can be completed by adding a phrase.

1. ______________________________, and I was knocked unconscious.

2. ______________________________, but the doctor couldn't save his life.

3. ______________________________ because we had a flat tire.

4. ______________________________, after the garage had been destroyed.

5. _________________________, when I suddenly noticed her standing there.

6. __________________________________ who put that package there?

7. When they were stopped by the police, ____________________________.

8. __________________________________ if you spend any more money.

9. Would Juan have bought that old car if ____________________________?

10. We would have sold it to him if ____________________________.

11. I suggest she ____________________________.

12. During ________________________________ I spent a lot of time in Italy.

13. __________________________________ because of the heat wave.

14. We found the wounded pilot, whose ____________________________.

15. Either you be on time, or ____________________________.

16. I wouldn't want to ____________________________.

17. Neither ________________ nor ________________ has any idea about it.

18. May I speak with ________________ when ____________________?

19. Maria is the only woman I ____________________________.

20. It's hard to believe that ____________________________.

If you have completed all the exercises in this chapter with a high degree of accuracy, you are ready to go on to the next stage of the writing program. If you feel you need more review, repeat the exercises that gave you trouble. Look at the Answer Key for suggestions for completing the sentences.

3

Writing Original Sentences

Understanding the Format

In Chapter 1 you worked with specific grammatical elements as a review of basic structures. In Chapter 2 you completed sentences with phrases that you created yourself. If you completed those two chapters successfully, you are ready to write original sentences of your own.

In this part of the writing program you will write short sentences using a given phrase. Each sentence you write should be in the form described. In the example sentences below, the indicated part of speech is in italics; note that it is not always the example phrase. Review the examples, but do not use the example sentences in your writing. If you are not sure how to proceed, look in the Answer Key for suggested ways of writing each sentence.

Example phrase: *the young barber*

HOW TO USE THAT PHRASE	EXAMPLE SENTENCES
A. subject of the sentence	*The young barber* fell down.
B. direct object	Mary likes *the young barber*.
C. indirect object	She gave *the young barber* a big tip.
D. object of a preposition	I got the bill from *the young barber*.
E. in a clause beginning with *because*	We were quiet *because the young barber was asleep*.
F. possessive *-'s*	*The young barber's* car needs to be repaired.
G. with an irregular past tense verb	The young barber *found* a kitten.
H. with an irregular present perfect tense verb	The young barber *has lost* his job.
I. with a verb in the past tense after the phrase *When he arrived*	When he arrived, the young barber *went* right to work.

J. with a verb in the present perfect tense with a present participle	The young barber *has been sweeping* up.
K. with a verb in the future perfect tense	The young barber *will have earned* fifty dollars by noon.
L. in a compound sentence with the conjunction *and*	The little girl picked out some candy, *and the young barber placed it in a bag.*
M. in a compound sentence with the conjunction *because*	The boss was angry *because the young barber was late again.*
N. antecedent of the relative pronoun *whose*	I met *the young barber,* whose girlfriend is an actress.
O. antecedent of the relative pronoun *that, who,* or *which*	Here is a photo of *the young barber* that used to work downtown.
P. antecedent of an elliptical relative pronoun	The woman thanked *the young barber* she liked so much.
Q. subject of a passive present perfect tense verb	The young barber *has been fired* today.
R. subject of a passive past tense verb	The young barber *was shocked* by the horrible news.
S. after a conditional phrase, such as *If he could hear me*	*If he could hear me,* the young barber would wave.

Writing According to the Format

Exercise 3.1 Write ten sentences similar to the examples in A–S. Next to the part of speech for each sentence you will see which example sentence is similar to your new sentence. Use the phrase *the new waiter.*

1. subject of the sentence (Compare to sample sentence A.)

____

2. direct object (Compare to sample sentence B.)

____

3. indirect object (Compare to sample sentence C.)

____

4. object of the preposition *for* (Compare to sample sentence D.)

____

5. object of the preposition *of* (Compare to sample sentence D.)

____

6. with an irregular present perfect tense verb (Compare to sample sentence H.)

____

7. with a verb in the future perfect tense (Compare to sample sentence K.)

____

8. in a compound sentence with the conjunction *and* (Compare to sample sentence L.)

____

9. antecedent of the relative pronoun *that* or *which* (Compare to sample sentence O.)

____

10. antecedent of an elliptical relative pronoun (Compare to sample sentence P.)

____

Exercise 3.2 Write ten sentences similar to the examples in A–S. Next to the part of speech for each sentence you will see which example sentence is similar to your new sentence. Use the phrase *some old friends.*

1. subject of the sentence (Compare to sample sentence A.)

____

2. direct object (Compare to sample sentence B.)

____

3. object of the preposition *to* (Compare to sample sentence D.)

____

4. object of the preposition *by* (Compare to sample sentence D.)

____

5. possessive (Compare to sample sentence F.)

____

6. with an irregular past tense verb (Compare to sample sentence G.)

____

7. in a compound sentence with the conjunction *because* (Compare to sample sentence M.)

____

8. antecedent of the relative pronoun *who* (Compare to sample sentence O.)

____

9. subject of a passive past tense verb (Compare to sample sentence R.)

____

10. after the conditional phrase *If she had loved me* (Compare to sample sentence S.)

____

Exercise 3.3 Write ten sentences similar to the examples in A–S. Next to the part of speech for each sentence you will see which example sentence is similar to your new sentence. Use the phrase *the new boss.*

1. subject of the sentence (Compare to sample sentence A.)

____

2. indirect object (Compare to sample sentence C.)

____

3. in a clause beginning with *because* (Compare to sample sentence E.)

____

4. object of the preposition *for* (Compare to sample sentence D.)

____

5. object of the preposition *from* (Compare to sample sentence D.)

____

6. in a compound sentence with the conjunction *and* (Compare to sample sentence L.)

____

7. in a compound sentence with the conjunction *because* (Compare to sample sentence M.)

____

8. subject of a passive present perfect tense verb (Compare to sample sentence Q.)

____

9. subject of a passive past tense verb (Compare to sample sentence R.)

____

10. after the conditional phrase *If you had helped us* (Compare to sample sentence S.)

____

Exercise 3.4 Write ten sentences similar to the examples in A–S. Next to the part of speech for each sentence you will see which example sentence is similar to your new sentence. Use the phrase *two dangerous criminals.*

1. subject of the sentence (Compare to sample sentence A.)

____

2. object of the preposition *into* (Compare to sample sentence D.)

____

3. object of the preposition *because of* (Compare to sample sentence D.)

____

4. possessive (Compare to sample sentence F.)

____

5. with a verb in the past tense after the phrase *When I saw him* (Compare to sample sentence I.)

____

6. with a verb in the present perfect tense with a present participle (Compare to sample sentence J.)

 ____

7. in a compound sentence with the conjunction *because* (Compare to sample sentence M.)

 ____

8. antecedent of the relative pronoun *who* (Compare to sample sentence O.)

 ____

9. subject of a passive present perfect tense verb (Compare to sample sentence Q.)

 ____

10. after the conditional phrase *If we had the money* (Compare to sample sentence S.)

 ____

Exercise 3.5 Write ten sentences similar to the examples in A–S. Next to the part of speech for each sentence you will see which example sentence is similar to your new sentence. Use the phrase *our Mexican guests.*

1. subject of the sentence (Compare to sample sentence A.)

 ____

2. direct object (Compare to sample sentence B.)

 ____

3. indirect object (Compare to sample sentence C.)

 ____

4. object of the preposition *to* (Compare to sample sentence D.)

____

5. object of the preposition *by* (Compare to sample sentence D.)

____

6. object of the preposition *instead of* (Compare to sample sentence D.)

____

7. with an irregular present perfect tense verb (Compare to sample sentence H.)

____

8. with a verb in the future perfect tense (Compare to sample sentence K.)

____

9. antecedent of the relative pronoun *that*, *who*, or *which* (Compare to sample sentence O.)

____

10. antecedent of an elliptical relative pronoun (Compare to sample sentence P.)

____

Exercise 3.6 Write ten sentences similar to the examples in A–S. Next to the part of speech for each sentence you will see which example sentence is similar to your new sentence. Use the phrase *the bravest woman*.

1. subject of the sentence (Compare to sample sentence A.)

____

2. object of the preposition *toward* (Compare to sample sentence D.)

____

3. object of the preposition *by* (Compare to sample sentence D.)

____

4. with an irregular present perfect tense verb (Compare to sample sentence H.)

____

5. antecedent of the relative pronoun *who* (Compare to sample sentence O.)

____

6. antecedent of the relative pronoun *that* or *which* (Compare to sample sentence O.)

____

7. antecedent of an elliptical relative pronoun (Compare to sample sentence P.)

____

8. subject of a passive present perfect tense verb (Compare to sample sentence Q.)

____

9. subject of a passive past tense verb (Compare to sample sentence R.)

____

10. after the conditional phrase *If he had lived longer* (Compare to sample sentence S.)

____

Exercise 3.7 Write ten sentences similar to the examples in A–S. Next to the part of speech for each sentence you will see which example sentence is similar to your new sentence. Use the phrase *a registered letter*.

1. direct object (Compare to sample sentence B.)

____

2. object of the preposition *without* (Compare to sample sentence D.)

____

3. object of the preposition *in spite of* (Compare to sample sentence D.)

____

4. object of the preposition *of* (Compare to sample sentence D.)

____

5. with a verb in the present perfect tense with a present participle (Compare to sample sentence J.)

____

6. with a verb in the future perfect tense (Compare to sample sentence K.)

____

7. in a compound sentence with the conjunction *and* (Compare to sample sentence L.)

____

8. in a compound sentence with the conjunction *because* (Compare to sample sentence M.)

____

9. antecedent of the relative pronoun *which* (Compare to sample sentence O.)

 ____

10. antecedent of the relative pronoun *that* (Compare to sample sentence O.)

 ____

Exercise 3.8 Write ten sentences similar to the examples in A–S. Next to the part of speech for each sentence you will see which example sentence is similar to your new sentence. Use the phrase *the proud parents.*

1. indirect object (Compare to sample sentence C.)

 ____

2. object of the preposition *because of* (Compare to sample sentence D.)

 ____

3. in a clause beginning with *because* (Compare to sample sentence E.)

 ____

4. with a verb in the present perfect tense with a present participle (Compare to sample sentence J.)

 ____

5. with a verb in the future perfect tense (Compare to sample sentence K.)

 ____

6. in a compound sentence with the conjunction *and* (Compare to sample sentence L.)

 ____

7. in a compound sentence with the conjunction *because* (Compare to sample sentence M.)

____

8. subject of a passive present perfect tense verb (Compare to sample sentence Q.)

____

9. subject of a passive past tense verb (Compare to sample sentence R.)

____

10. after the conditional phrase *If it had snowed* (Compare to sample sentence S.)

____

Exercise 3.9 Write ten sentences similar to the examples in A–S. Next to the part of speech for each sentence you will see which example sentence is similar to your new sentence. Use the phrase *his youngest daughter*.

1. subject of the sentence (Compare to sample sentence A.)

____

2. indirect object (Compare to sample sentence C.)

____

3. object of the preposition *down* (Compare to sample sentence D.)

____

4. with an irregular past tense verb (Compare to sample sentence G.)

____

5. with a verb in the past tense after the phrase *When I saw him* (Compare to sample sentence I.)

____

6. with a verb in the future perfect tense (Compare to sample sentence K.)

____

7. in a compound sentence with the conjunction *because* (Compare to sample sentence M.)

____

8. antecedent of the relative pronoun *who* (Compare to sample sentence O.)

____

9. subject of a passive present perfect tense verb (Compare to sample sentence Q.)

____

10. after the conditional phrase *If I had been wrong* (Compare to sample sentence S.)

____

Exercise 3.10 Write ten sentences similar to the examples in A–S. Next to the part of speech for each sentence you will see which example sentence is similar to your new sentence. Use the phrase *an angry mob.*

1. object of the preposition *to* (Compare to sample sentence D.)

____

2. object of the preposition *because of* (Compare to sample sentence D.)

____

3. object of the preposition *from* (Compare to sample sentence D.)

____

4. possessive (Compare to sample sentence F.)

____

5. with an irregular present perfect tense verb (Compare to sample sentence H.)

____

6. with a verb in the present perfect tense with a present participle (Compare to sample sentence J.)

____

7. in a compound sentence with the conjunction *and* (Compare to sample sentence L.)

____

8. object of the preposition *about* (Compare to sample sentence D.)

____

9. antecedent of an elliptical relative pronoun (Compare to sample sentence P.)

____

10. subject of a passive past tense verb (Compare to sample sentence R.)

____

Exercise 3.11 Write ten sentences similar to the examples in A–S. Next to the part of speech for each sentence you will see which example sentence is similar to your new sentence. Use the phrase *several pretty girls.*

1. subject of the sentence (Compare to sample sentence A.)

   ____

2. indirect object (Compare to sample sentence C.)

   ____

3. in a clause beginning with *because* (Compare to sample sentence E.)

   ____

4. object of the preposition *toward* (Compare to sample sentence D.)

   ____

5. with an irregular past tense verb (Compare to sample sentence G.)

   ____

6. with an irregular present perfect tense verb (Compare to sample sentence H.)

   ____

7. with a verb in the past tense after the phrase *When I met him* (Compare to sample sentence I.)

   ____

8. in a compound sentence with the conjunction *because* (Compare to sample sentence M.)

   ____

9. antecedent of an elliptical relative pronoun (Compare to sample sentence P.)

   ____

10. after the conditional phrase *If he had seen her* (Compare to sample sentence S.)

____

Exercise 3.12 Write ten sentences similar to the examples in A–S. Next to the part of speech for each sentence you will see which example sentence is similar to your new sentence. Use the phrase *the drunken soldier*.

1. indirect object (Compare to sample sentence C.)

____

2. object of the preposition *besides* (Compare to sample sentence D.)

____

3. in a clause beginning with *because* (Compare to sample sentence E.)

____

4. object of the preposition *around* (Compare to sample sentence D.)

____

5. with an irregular past tense verb (Compare to sample sentence G.)

____

6. with an irregular present perfect tense verb (Compare to sample sentence H.)

____

7. with a verb in the present perfect tense with a present participle (Compare to sample sentence J.)

____

8. in a compound sentence with the conjunction *because* (Compare to sample sentence M.)

____

9. subject of a passive present perfect tense verb (Compare to sample sentence Q.)

____

10. after the conditional phrase *If it had rained* (Compare to sample sentence S.)

____

Exercise 3.13 Write ten sentences similar to the examples in A–S. Next to the part of speech for each sentence you will see which example sentence is similar to your new sentence. Use the phrase *his driver's license.*

1. object of the preposition *on* (Compare to sample sentence D.)

____

2. in a clause beginning with *because* (Compare to sample sentence E.)

____

3. object of the preposition *from* (Compare to sample sentence D.)

____

4. with an irregular present perfect tense verb (Compare to sample sentence H.)

____

5. with a verb in the present perfect tense with a present participle (Compare to sample sentence J.)

____

6. in a compound sentence with the conjunction *and* (Compare to sample sentence L.)

____

7. in a compound sentence with the conjunction *because* (Compare to sample sentence M.)

____

8. antecedent of the relative pronoun *that* or *which* (Compare to sample sentence O.)

____

9. subject of a passive present perfect tense verb (Compare to sample sentence Q.)

____

10. after the conditional phrase *If she had seen us* (Compare to sample sentence S.)

____

Exercise 3.14 Write ten sentences similar to the examples in A–S. Next to the part of speech for each sentence you will see which example sentence is similar to your new sentence. Use the phrase *the best candidates*.

1. subject of the sentence (Compare to sample sentence A.)

____

2. direct object (Compare to sample sentence B.)

____

3. indirect object (Compare to sample sentence C.)

____

4. object of the preposition *in spite of* (Compare to sample sentence D.)

____

5. possessive (Compare to sample sentence F.)

____

6. with an irregular past tense verb (Compare to sample sentence G.)

____

7. with an irregular present perfect tense verb (Compare to sample sentence H.)

____

8. with a verb in the past tense after the phrase *When I found them* (Compare to sample sentence I.)

____

9. with a verb in the present perfect tense with a present participle (Compare to sample sentence J.)

____

10. with a verb in the future perfect tense (Compare to sample sentence K.)

____

Exercise 3.15 Write ten sentences similar to the examples in A–S. Next to the part of speech for each sentence you will see which example sentence is similar to your new sentence. Use the phrase *the bride and groom.*

1. direct object (Compare to sample sentence B.)

____

2. possessive (Compare to sample sentence F.)

____

3. with an irregular past tense verb (Compare to sample sentence G.)

____

4. with an irregular present perfect tense verb (Compare to sample sentence H.)

____

5. with a verb in the past tense after the phrase *When he hit me* (Compare to sample sentence I.)

____

6. antecedent of the relative pronoun *whose* (Compare to sample sentence N.)

____

7. antecedent of the relative pronoun *that* or *which* (Compare to sample sentence O.)

____

8. antecedent of an elliptical relative pronoun (Compare to sample sentence P.)

____

9. subject of a passive present perfect tense verb (Compare to sample sentence Q.)

____

10. after the conditional phrase *If you had lied to me* (Compare to sample sentence S.)

____

4

Story Completion

Understanding the Format

In this section of the writing program you will write a variety of stories. But you do not have to make up the entire story. Parts of it are provided. You fill in the missing phrases that make sense in the sentence and that follow the story line. Although the story conforms to a certain idea, you can be creative and give the details that put your personal touch on the story.

This kind of exercise will give you the practice you need for the time when you eventually write a complete story on your own.

Study the story in each exercise, and take note of the missing phrases. Certain words will give you a signal as to what kind of word or phrase you should write. A conjunction, for example, tells you to add a word, phrase, or sentence. Quotation marks tell you that someone is making a direct statement. Prepositions require an object after them.

You should fill in appropriate phrases that conform to the plot of the story and the grammar of the sentence. Be careful of tenses and spelling. Follow the same directions for each story in this chapter. If you are not satisfied with your version of the story, check the suggested completions in the Answer Key.

Completing Stories with Original Phrases

Exercise 4.1 *Travel Plans.* The story line: John and Mary can't agree on where they should take their vacation. They share their personal preferences and try to persuade each other. They worry that they can't afford a vacation, but John has a surprise. He has saved some extra money.

John and Mary wanted to take a vacation. They had worked hard all year and ______________________________. But where should they go? To ______________________________ or to ______________________________?

"I want to go to Mexico," Mary said. "I heard it's ______________________________ and ______________________________."

"I think I'd like to go to India," John replied. "I want to see ______________________________ and ______________________________."

"India is so far away," Mary said to him. "I think ______________________________. Or we could travel to ______________________________."

"Or how about ______________________________?" John said.

But no matter how much they talked, they couldn't ______________________________. John believed ______________________________, but Mary wanted ______________________________. How could they decide what would be best for both of them?

John opened the newspaper and saw ______________________________. He showed Mary the article, and she ______________________________.

"That sounds like fun," Mary said. "I'd love ______________________________."

"We could swim during the day, and at night ______________ ______________ or ______________,"
John said. "And we could go shopping ______________."

Mary was happy with the idea, because ______________ ______________ and ______________.
John wouldn't mind spending time at the beach, because he knew ______________. But there still was a problem.

"______________?" Mary suddenly asked. "Do we have enough in the bank?"

John thought a moment, and then he ______________ ______________. He opened the desk drawer and ______________ ______________. He showed Mary ______________ ______________, but she ______________.
John smiled at her and said, "Don't worry. ______________ ______________. And if it's not enough, we can ______________."

"Oh, John," Mary said happily. "Now ______________ ______________. This vacation ______________."

Then he kissed her cheek, because ______________ ______________.

Exercise 4.2 *The Ant and the Grasshopper.* The story line: An ant is busy working to prepare for winter. A grasshopper is lazy and just enjoying himself. The ant warns the grasshopper that the sunny days will come to an end. When winter comes, the grasshopper learns just how right the ant was.

It was a beautiful summer day. The sky ________________________ ____________________, and the field was filled with ____________________ ________________________. A happy, green grasshopper with long legs and ____ jumped from a bouncy leaf to ____ and ____. He was enjoying the wonderful weather. He sang to himself, as he ________________________ ________________________.

Then he saw a small black ant near ____________________________ ________________________. She was pulling a crust of bread through ____. She tugged and pulled, but ____. Then the ant stopped for a moment to rest and ____. "Why are you doing that?" the grasshopper asked. "________________ ________________________?" he inquired with a laugh.

"I'm bringing food to our colony," the little ant replied. "When winter comes, ____."

"Winter is a long way off," the grasshopper said. "I'd rather ______ ______________________________."

"You might be sorry when ______________________________," the ant warned. "You should plan for ______________________."

But the grasshopper just laughed and ____________________ ______________. He jumped over ______________________ and hopped across ______________________________, playing, singing, and ______________________________.

The little ant shook her head and went back to work. She ______ ______________________________ and finally ______________ ______________.

The grasshopper saw the ant working nearly every day. And every day he just ______________________________. Soon it began to grow cold. The wind ______________________________. The snow ______________________________. And the grasshopper understood ______________________________. He made his way to the ant colony and called out, "______________ ______________." But the ants could not hear him. They ______________________________________, and the poor grasshopper ______________________________.

Exercise 4.3 *I'm No Cook!* The story line: A man is taking care of his children and his house by himself. He wants to make a nice supper for his children. Although he prepares the foods carefully, he makes some mistakes, and the family has to go to a restaurant for dinner.

My wife was called away to New York on business. I took some vacation time and ______________________________. Our two kids were in school during the day, and ______________________________. They were old enough to take care of themselves, but I had to ______________________________. John was eleven and spent his time ______________________________. Anne was ten and enjoyed sports like ______________________________.

Everything started out smoothly the first day. I cleaned the kitchen and ______________________________. I ironed ______________________________ and took the dog ______________________________. And for lunch I made myself ______________________________. The kids ate lunch ______________________________, because ______________________________.

At four o'clock I realized that the kids ______________________________, so I decided to ______________________________. I got a recipe book from the shelf and found ______________________________

________________. It seemed easy enough, although ____________ ________________________. I got the ingredients I needed out of the cupboard: ____.

I started with the salad. I rinsed a head of lettuce and then _____ ________________________________. I sliced __________________ ____________________ and scattered them over the lettuce. But I forgot to ____________________________________. I peeled a cucumber and an onion and ______________________________. I sprinkled ______________________________ over the salad and went to place it in the refrigerator. But when I placed the bowl on the shelf in the refrigerator, the shelf broke and ____________________________.

I couldn't believe my eyes. There were ______________________ ____________ on the floor and _________________________________ on my shoes. I grabbed a broom and _________________________. Then I got a bucket and scrub brush in order to _______________ __________________. When I was done, I sat down and _______ ______________________________________.

The roast looked easier to prepare. I placed it in a large pan and covered it ______________________________________. I sprinkled salt and pepper ____ and ________________________________. I peeled three potatoes and six ______________________ and ______________________. Before I put the roast in the oven, I checked the shelf. I didn't want ________________________________. Then I carefully put the roast in the oven and ________________________________.

For dessert I made vanilla ice cream with ________________ ________________. That was Anne's favorite, and John ________ ______________________. I put the three bowls of dessert on the counter. About four-thirty ______________________________. They went to their rooms to ____________________________.

I set the table and then called ____________________________. They hurried into the kitchen and took their seats. John was hungry, and Anne ________________________. But something had gone wrong. I hadn't put the dessert in the refrigerator, and __________ ________________________! And I had forgotten to turn on the oven, so the roast ________________________________!

The kids looked sad and ________________________________. So we got in the car, and I took them ________________________ __________. We all love tacos and fajitas.

Exercise 4.4 *The Circle of Stones.* The story line: Two women claim to be the mother of a lost child. A judge has to decide which woman is the real mother. By using a test he discovers which woman treats the child the most kindly and awards her the child.

This was the strangest case the judge had ever had. A child had been lost for ________________________________ and ________ ________________________. The poor child did not know its real mother, because ________________________________. Two women claimed to be the real mother and demanded ____________ ____________________. The judge needed more information first and ________________________________.

The first woman told of ____________________________, when ____________________________. The judge understood but asked, "____________________________?" The first woman just shook her head and ________________________. Now the second woman gave her story, which ______________ ______________. She explained that ____________________ ____________________, and the judge believed her. But who is the real mother? the judge thought. He looked at the child and asked, "______________________________?" But the sobbing child could only reply, "________________________________."

"Then we shall have a test," the judge said ______________________ ______________________. He placed the child in a ring of stones and told the two women ______________________. Each took the child by one hand, and ______________________. They pulled to the right and then ______________________, and the child began ______________________.

The women pulled again, but ______________________. Finally the first woman saw her chance and ______________________ ______________________. The child fell forward and ______________________ ______________________. The first woman laughed and proclaimed, "______________________." The second woman began to sob, because ______________________. And the child sat on the ground, shaking and ______________________.

The judge stood up and said, "______________________, because the second woman would not harm the child. Therefore I am certain that ______________________."

He gave the child to the second woman and sent the first woman ______________________. The child had been reunited with its rightful mother, who ______________________.

Exercise 4.5 *The Joke.* The story line: A boy takes a girl sledding. As they zoom down a hill, he whispers affectionately in her ear. But she is not certain what she hears. Later she marries and moves away. When she is old, she returns to her hometown and plays the same trick on her friend from the past.

It was a cold day in ______________________________. Victor and Lara were school friends and decided ________________ ________________. The snow was fresh and the hill was inviting, so they pulled their sled ______________________________. When ______________________________, he sat behind Lara and ______________________________. They went slowly at first, but ______________________________ and ________ ______________________________. They built up speed, and by now ______________________________. Lara screamed with delight, and Victor ______________________________. He liked Lara a lot but was afraid ______________________________. He wasn't shy, but ______________________________. So, as they whizzed down the hill, he thought of a joke that ____________ ________________. As the air rushed past their ears, Victor leaned forward and whispered, "______________________________." Lara didn't seem to hear him, so ______________________________. And he said in a rush, "I love you, Lara." She began to blush. She wasn't sure ________________________________. Was it the wind? Was _______________________________? Was it Victor?

At the bottom of the hill, Victor looked at Lara, who __________ _________________________. But he only smiled and __________ _________________________. He could not say how he felt and only _______________________________.

They grew up, and Lara went __________________________. While living there, she _______________________________. When she returned to her hometown many years later, she learned that Victor ________________________________. They were both old now and _______________________________. Lara decided it was time for _______________________________.

She saw Victor sitting _______________________________ near a fence. She came up behind him on the other side of the fence and ________________________________. She peeked at him __________________________________. And through a wide crack in one of the boards, Lara __________________________, "I _______________________________." The wind was blowing hard and _______________________________. The leaves were rustling above _______________________________. Victor wasn't sure he had heard correctly. "________________________

__________?" he asked, looking around. But there was no answer. Lara stood silently ______________________________. Then she ______________________________ and said in a whisper, "I love you, too, Victor."

The joke was on ______________________________.

Exercise 4.6 *The Worst Day of My Life.* The story line: A man is driving to visit some friends in another city. But he has many problems. His car stalls. It starts to rain. He gets splattered with mud. And he loses his money. Worst of all, his friends are not at home.

Everyone has a bad day now and then. But I had the worst. It happened while I was visiting ______________________________. They were old friends of mine and had just moved to ______________________________. I loved spending time in a big city and was looking forward to ______________________________.

I left my hometown around ______________________________ and arrived ______________________________ around dusk. Before I found my friends' new house, my car ______________________________. I thought I was out of gas, but ______________________________. I wasn't sure what to do. I finally decided to ______________________________. I thought I had seen a gas station there, but ______________________________. I thought I had better call my friends. I found a telephone booth and ______________________________, but no one ______________________________.

Just as I began to walk back to my car, it ______________________________. I was soaked to the skin by ______________________________. I tried starting my car again, but ______________________________. When it finally stopped raining, I got out of the car to ______________________________. As I stepped in front of the car, a truck zoomed by and ______________________________. My clothes were drenched again, and my face ______________________________. I sputtered and cursed the truck, just as a car ______________________________.

By now I was shivering from being so wet and from ______________________________. Late fall can be ______________________________. I began to walk along the road in the direction of some bright lights. But I stepped in a puddle of mud and lost ______________________________. I searched for ______________________________, but it was buried in mud. So I limped on, wearing ______________________________. Then the heel fell off of it, and now I was limping ___________________________________.

Finally I had some good luck. A taxi came by, and ____________ ______________________________. Once I got inside the taxi, I began to warm up. I told the driver ____. I didn't realize how far it still was to their house. When I arrived at their house, ____. When I reached into my pocket, I discovered ____________________________________. I had no money! I was soaking wet! And I was tired!

I ran to my friends' door and rang the bell, but ______________ ____________________________. Then I found a note for me taped to the door. It read, "____. We'll see you when we get back."

I sat on the wet porch and cried. It was the worst day of my life.

Exercise 4.7 *The Desert.* The story line: A family moves out West. The brother loves riding his pony. The sister loves playing in the desert. One day the sister gets lost, and the brother rides out to find her. When he discovers her, he sees something dangerous crawling in her direction. The boy saves his sister.

Jimmy was only eight when his parents ____________________ _______________________________. They moved to a large ranch near

______________________________. It was a wonderful place to live, but ______________________________. Jimmy liked ______________________________ and thought the West was just ______________________________.

His little sister, Laura, was five and loved ______________________________. She often played in the desert and ______________________________. Jimmy warned her not to ______________________________, but Laura ______________________________.

One day Laura ______________________________, which was very far from their house. When she didn't come home for lunch, everyone ______________________________. Jimmy was very worried. He got on his pony and ______________________________. He rode as far as ______________________________. Then he ______________________________. By three o'clock he had ridden ______________________________, but he couldn't ______________________________. He was ready to cry or even ______________________________.

Then he saw it! It was a large ______________________________, where Laura often ______________________________. He rode up to ______________________________. And there was

Laura asleep next to ______________________________. She didn't see ______________________________, which was crawling in her direction. Jimmy jumped from his pony and ______________________________. He took his lasso, swirled it overhead, and then ______________________________. He missed! He had to try again, so he ______________________________, and this time he ______________________________ and saved his sister.

Exercise 4.8 *The Hero.* The story line: A girl lives with her grandfather in a cozy house. One cold day they build a fire in the fireplace. It's very warm in the room and they fall asleep. The girl wakes up to see that the fire has spread into the room. She puts out the fire and saves her grandfather.

In winter it gets very cold in ______________________________, because it's located near ______________________________. A lot of snow falls to the ground, and a lot of ______________________________.

Little Anna's house stays warm and ______________________________, because ______________________________. There is a large fireplace in the dining room, where her grandfather ______________________________. Anna loves ______________________________, while her grandfather ______________________________.

One chilly December day, when ______________________________ ______________, Grandfather noticed the fire ______________ ______________. He went out to the barn and returned with ______________________________. Anna liked helping and ______________________________________. Soon the fire ______________________________. The dining room glowed with ______________________________. The shadows on the walls ______________________________, and everything in the house was ______________________________. Grandfather sat in his big, old armchair and soon ______________________. He put his feet on ______________________________. Anna curled up on the floor under ______________________________. Everything was quiet and ______________________________.

Anna suddenly opened her eyes. Something was wrong! She smelled ______________________________! She saw ______________ ______________ and ______________________________! She jumped up and ______________________________. The fire was no longer just in the fireplace. ______________ ______________________________! Anna shook her grandfather, but ______________________________. She ran to the sink and ____________________________________. She began throwing water ____________________________________. Finally the fire was out, and ____________________________________. When Grandfather awoke, he said, "____________________________________."

Anna just shook her head and smiled.

Exercise 4.9 *The Pickpocket.* The story line: A thief is watching the crowds of people on the street. When he sees an easy victim, he sneaks up and steals the victim's wallet or purse. Finally a policewoman sees what he is doing and arrests him. The policewoman finds what the thief has stolen, and the man is sent to jail.

It was a hot day, and ____________________________________. People enjoyed holiday time like this and ____________________ ____________________________. It was a happy time for Mike because ____________________________________. Mike knew there would be a lot of pockets that ____________________________________. The crowds were enormous, and everyone ____________________ ________________. Mike couldn't have been happier if ________________ ____________________. When ________________________________, he walked slowly down the street and __________________________ ______________. Finally he saw ____________________________________, who ____________________________________. He came up behind her and carefully ________________________________. The poor woman was aware of nothing and ____________________ ____________________. Her husband turned suddenly, but Mike ______________________________. On the corner Mike saw ______________________________, who ______________ ____________________. Mike stood next to ______________ ______________ and then ______________________________. He pulled out ______________________________. Mike smiled; he was very happy with himself and ______________ ______________________________.

When he ______________________________, Mike decided ______________________________ and ______________________________. He got away that time and knew ______________________________. But the policewoman ______________________________. Mike couldn't see ______________________________ and ______________ ______________________________. When he slid his fingers into ______________________________, he was surprised ______________ ____________________. The policewoman had been watching him and ______________________________. Mike dropped

____________________________ and tried ______________________________ ______________. But the policewoman had __________________________ ________________; Mike was caught. He knew he couldn't get away now and said, "______________________________________." The policewoman just laughed and replied, "____."

When they got to ____, the officers there found ______________________________________. Trying to explain, Mike said, "____." But no one believed him. For the next few months Mike ____________ ____.

Exercise 4.10 *Laddy to the Rescue.* The story line: When a little girl goes for a walk, she soon finds that she is lost. She becomes frightened by a noise in an empty house and runs off to hide. Her dog senses that something has happened to her and hurries out to look for her. Finally he finds her and leads her home, where he receives a reward.

During ____, a seven-year-old girl decided to go for a walk. She went __________________________ ______________________ and soon realized that she was lost. She looked around her, but ____.

She began crying, and ____. But ____. The little girl walked along the wide path bordered with ____________________. Soon ____________________, and the little girl walked faster. There in the distance she could see ____________________. She opened the door and ____________________. There was a sudden, horrible noise, and ____________________. She ran and ran and found herself alone in ____________________. She was terribly lonely and afraid, so ____________________. Cold and tired, she fell asleep near ____________________.

The little girl had a large, shaggy dog named Laddy. He was loyal to her and sensed that ____________________. There was no way out of the house, so Laddy ____________________. He ran to ____________________; he looked in ____________________, but Laddy couldn't ____________________. Suddenly there was a familiar scent on the ground. Laddy lowered his head and ____________________. He looked right and left. He barked ____________________. Then Laddy ____________________ until he found

______________________________________. But the strange little house was empty. Laddy looked around and ________________ __________________. Something caught his eye; Laddy suddenly saw ______________________________________. He jumped over some bushes and __________________________________. A few moments later he saw ______________________________, where the little girl ________________________________. When she saw her dog standing over her, she said, "____________________ __________________," and ____________________________________.

Laddy led his little mistress _____________________________ and ___________________________________. Mother and Father were so relieved. And that night Laddy ________________________________.

Exercise 4.11 *The Day I Got Fired.* The story line: A man has a job in a factory. His foreman doesn't like him and treats him poorly. When the man arrives late for work one day, the foreman threatens to fire him. And when the man ruins an important job, he does get fired. Fortunately, he has a better job now.

I finally found a good job in ____________________________ __________________. The company made electronics for _______________ ______________________________________. I was put on a line where ______________________________________, and I had to ____________

______________________________. The job was rather simple, and I believed I was doing well. Then they hired a new foreman, who ______________________________. For some reason he didn't like me and often said, "______________________________." I was afraid of him because he could ______________________ __________. And I needed my job. Without a job I ___________ ______________________________.

I knew I had to be careful around the foreman and __________ ______________________. Then one day my car ___________ ________________, and I arrived ______________________. The foreman was ______________________________ and began shouting at me. When I explained that ______________________ ___________, he just laughed and ______________________ __________. I went to my job and began __________________ ____________. I worked hard and tried to _______________ ______________________________.

When lunchtime finally arrived, I sat at a table with __________ ______________________. She was a really nice woman and told me ______________________________. But it wouldn't be easy to get along with him, because he ______________________________.

After lunch I started soldering some new circuit boards. They had to be shipped to ________________________. I was hurrying because ________________________. But I worked too fast and ruined ________________________. The foreman was furious with me. He said, "________________________!" Then he pointed at the door and shouted, "________________________!"

I never went back there again. And now I have a better job, and my boss is ________________________.

Exercise 4.12 *The Blind Date.* The story line: A young man decides that it's time to date again after ending a long relationship. His friend sets him up with a blind date. The young man and woman discover they have a lot in common and begin dating regularly. Finally they decide to marry and start a family.

I had been going out with Barbara for more than ________________________. But we had some problems and decided ________________________. We're still friends, and we often get together to ________________________.

Several months went by after we broke up, and I ________________________. It was getting boring sitting at home and ________________________. Then my friend Bill suggested I go out on a blind date. I had never ____________________ ________ and wasn't sure that a blind date ____________________ ______________. But I agreed, and Bill ____________________ ______________________________.

He arranged for me to meet ____________________________. She was a friend of his from work. He said she ______________ ______________ and ____________________________. I like women who ____________________________, so I was interested to meet her. At eight p.m. on Saturday, I left home and ______________________________. I went in and took a seat near ______________________. About ten minutes later a woman who ______________________ came in and began to look around. I knew ____________________________.

She took a seat across from me and said, "______________ ______________." I was flattered because she ____________ __________________. We chatted a while and then ordered some dinner. She had quite an appetite and ________________ __________. I had never seen a woman eat so much. "I like to cook," she finally said, "and I ____________________________."

The evening went by quickly because ____________________

____________________. I didn't think I could fall in love so fast, but

______________________________________. We went out several

times during the next ______________________________________,

and when spring came we were inseparable. I finally bought ________

____________________________, and on June first I __________

____________________________. To my amazement she immediately

said, "____________________________________."

After a yearlong engagement, we ________________________

________. Now we have a house and ____________________________

and a third on the way. I have never been happier and believe that

____________________________________.

Who could have known that a blind date ____________________

________________________________.

Exercise 4.13 *No More Used Cars!* The story line: A woman wants to buy a used car because she cannot afford a new car. She finally finds one that looks good, but it doesn't run well. It breaks down regularly. Finally the woman pays for a tune-up, and the car runs better. But she hopes she doesn't have to buy another used car.

Buying a new car is expensive. That's why I ________________

__________________. I would love to own a new car, but for now

________________________________. Last winter my old car finally died. I tried to start it, but ________________________________. I sold it for junk and went to buy ____________________________.

I had seen the Johnson's Pre-Owned Vehicles lot __________________________________ and decided to stop there to __________________________________. Some of the cars were just too old, and others __________________________________. I had to make a compromise between __________________________________ and __________________________________. I finally found a __________________________________ with a little rust on it, but it seemed to run ______________________________.

I paid Mr. Johnson with a check, signed __________________________________, and drove home __________________________________. I was rather proud of my new vehicle. It looked __________________________ and sounded __________________________________. My brother was impressed with my purchase and said, "__________________________________." But my father was skeptical. He laughed and said to me, "Used cars __________________________________."

My "new" car ran well for a long time. Then on a very cold morning in January, I went to the garage and ______________________ ___________. But the car ___________________________________. It was frustrating. It just wouldn't start. My brother came out to the garage and ________________________________. Finally the motor was running, and I _______________________________. I arrived at work late and explained that ______________________ _____________________________.

When five o'clock came and I was ready ___________________ _______________, I went out to the parking lot to start my car. And again ___________________________________. Now I was mad. Really mad! I looked at that car and shouted, "_________________ _________________!" Naturally, the car couldn't understand what I said and just ________________________________. One of my coworkers was watching me and ____________________________. It was pretty embarrassing.

It took half an hour to start that car, but it __________________ ____________________. I wish it had never started. Two blocks from work the engine ______________________________________, and I

was stuck in the middle of the street. I got it started again, and two blocks later the radiator ________________________________.
That old car stalled five times on the way home.

When I finally arrived there, my family was ________________ ________________. They knew something was wrong with my car because ____________________________. My father laughed again and said, "Don't buy a used car unless ____________ ____________________." I knew he was right and got a tune-up the next day.

My car wasn't perfect after that, but it ____________________.
And I learned a lesson: if you're going to buy a used car, you had better ____________________________. As for me, I hope to get rich and never ____________________________.

Exercise 4.14 *Computers Can Be Dumb.* The story line: A man has to use a computer in his new job. But the computer acts like the man's enemy. It makes mistakes and provides wrong information. The man is eventually fired. But a few days later he is rehired because the management discovered that the computer was faulty.

I was always afraid of computers. They ____________________ ____________ and made me feel ________________________.
Of course, they are just machines and can't ____________________

________________. But I always felt that they were trying to make me look foolish.

When I got a job in a warehouse, I had to learn ________________ ______________________. It's not what I wanted to do, but it was part of the job. So I reluctantly ____________________________________. In time, I thought I had mastered _______________________________, but the truth was that the computer _________________________________. As I gained more experience, the computer seemed to make more mistakes. I'd type in one number, and the computer __________________ _____________________. I complained to my boss that the computer I was using ____. He laughed and told me to ______________________________________.

Then for a few weeks everything went fine. I ____________________ ____________________, and the computer ______________________ __________________. But then it began. I'd come to work and turn on the computer, and ____. I couldn't believe my eyes. How could _______________________________ happen? Where did ____ come from? I didn't type in those things. I knew it was the computer trying ____.

Finally my boss came to me with some complaints from management. He asked, "________________________________?" I said it wasn't my fault, and once again he laughed and said, "________________________________." No one believed me. Why would anyone believe that ________________________________? It was too incredible.

Then I got the news. The manager sent word to my boss that ________________________________. The next day I got my final paycheck. My boss said my work had too many mistakes and ________________________________. He told me to ________________________________. I went home and felt ________________________________.

Two days later I got a telephone call. It was the manager. He said that ________________________________ and that I could have my job back. It turned out that the computer ________________________________; it had a defective motherboard. I was so happy that I ________________________________.

I returned to work the next day and sat down to a new computer. This one was friendly, and we ________________________________.

Exercise 4.15 *How I Became a Millionaire.* The story line: A woman receives the news that she has won a large sum of money. She and her friend go on a buying spree and live like royalty. Her friend suggests she put some of her money in the bank. After enjoying her riches for only a short time, the woman wakes up. It was all a dream.

Many people dream about becoming rich and living ____________ ______________________________. They hope they'll win ____________ ______________________________ or inherit ______________________ ______________. But it doesn't work out that way for most.

One morning I got out of bed and ran down the stairs to get the mail. I had a feeling that ____________________________________. And I was right. Among the letters I found was ________________ ________________. It stated that I ________________________ ____________. I couldn't believe my eyes. I had won ____________ ______________________! I was a millionaire!

I called my best friend, Anna, who ______________________ ______________. She was as excited as I was and ________________ ______________________. She asked, "______________________ ____________?" And she asked, "______________________________ ________________?" I didn't know the answer. Where do you begin to spend money, when ______________________________________?

I was new at this, but I ____.
You learn some things fast.

Anna and I went downtown, but not on the bus. We ________
____, and on the way home I rented
____. I felt like a queen. I could
afford anything I wanted, and I wanted ____________________
____________. But Anna was wiser than me. She suggested ________
________________________________ and ____________________
____________. I realized that was smart and decided I would put some
money ________________________________. But I would spend
the rest on ________________________________. Why not? I
was a millionaire!

I bought several new dresses for myself, and for Anna ________
____________________________. She was elated and said, "________
____." We both loved shoes, so
____. And I stocked up on
____________________________ and ____________________________.
I was on a buying spree, and ________________________________.

But something did stop me. It didn't seem possible. It ________
________________________________. I was being tricked. Fate had

____________________________________. It wasn't fair, and I lowered my head ____________________________________. It wasn't fair!

I had been a millionaire for ______________________________. Just like so many others, I had only dreamed it. My wealth was just ____________________________________.

5

Writing Letters

The Friendly Letter

The friendly letter is exactly what you'd think it would be: a casual letter that is sent to a friend. The style is *informal*, and the content is *personal*. It reads very much like what you would be saying if you were chatting with a friend. The content can be intimate or informative or can even be a request. It is up to you, the writer, to put the thoughts on paper that you wish to send to a friend.

There are some simple rules to follow when writing a friendly letter:

- Put the date at the upper left or right of the page. You may add your address below the date, but it is optional.

  June 30, 2003
  2990 West Main Street
  Johnstown, IL 60622

- Begin with a greeting. You can show affection or love in the greeting.

  Dear Mary,
  Dearest Mom and Dad,
  My beloved Mary,

- Next, begin the body of your letter. The content is up to you.

  I have missed you . . .

- Close the letter at the lower right or left. You can express affection or love in the closing as in the opening.

  Sincerely yours,
  Affectionately,
  With all my love,

- End the letter by signing your name.

  Bill

- You can add a postscript with a final thought at the very end.
  P.S.

Notice that the greeting and the closing are followed by a comma (for example, "Dear Mary," and "Sincerely yours,").

Look at the three possibilities for the greeting of a friendly letter. Greetings can be friendly, affectionate, or loving:

FRIENDLY GREETINGS	AFFECTIONATE GREETINGS	LOVING GREETINGS
Dear Mary,	My Dearest Mary,	My Beloved Mary,
My Dear Mary,	Dearest Mary,	My Darling Mary,
Hello, Mary,	My Dearest,	My Sweet,
Hi, Mary,	Dearest,	My Darling,
		Darling,

There are similar possibilities for the closing of a friendly letter:

FRIENDLY CLOSINGS	AFFECTIONATE CLOSINGS	LOVING CLOSINGS
Sincerely,	Fondly,	Love,
Sincerely yours,	Affectionately,	Lovingly,
Truly,	With fond regards,	With all my love,
Truly yours,	With sincere affection,	I love you,
Yours truly,		
Yours sincerely,		

Naturally, what's considered a friendly, an affectionate, or a loving greeting and closing in a friendly letter may vary from person to person. But you can rely on the ones just listed to help you open and close a friendly letter with the degree of friendship, affection, or love you wish to express.

Now let's look at a sample of a friendly letter. This sample will express simple friendship between a man and a woman.

June 30, 2004

2990 West Main Street
Johnstown, IL 60622

Dear Mary,

I'm sorry I haven't written sooner, but I've been away on the most wonderful trip. My friend Bill and I rented a van and traveled from Johnstown to Seattle, then from Seattle to Los Angeles, and returned home by way of the Grand Canyon.

It was the most spectacular trip. We saw mountain ranges, beautiful forestlands, deserts, and the magnificent Grand Canyon. I never expected the Grand Canyon to be so big or to be so breathtaking. Bill took several hundred pictures, and I, of course, had my video camera running all the time. I'm eager to show you what we saw.

The only bad moment came when Bill sprained his ankle hiking down a trail. I carried him piggyback all the way back to the van. We must have been quite a sight. We both laughed for a long time, even though Bill was in a lot of pain. Two days later his ankle was a lot better, and by the time we reached Johnstown, he was as right as rain.

I wish you could have been with us. But you'll have to experience our adventure through our pictures. Let's get together soon.

I hope you're well and that things are going smoothly at your new job. I look forward to seeing you.

Yours truly,
Jim

P.S. If you want to call me, I have a new cell phone number: 555-1234.

Exercise 5.1 Compose a friendly letter by filling in each of the following boxes with the suggested information. Put two or three sentences in each of the three boxes in the body of the letter.

Date Address

Greeting

Write about something you recently bought

Write about a trip you would like to take

Write about something that happened to a family member

Closing

Sign your name

Exercise 5.2 Compose a friendly letter by filling in each of the following boxes with the suggested information. Put two or three sentences in each of the three boxes in the body of the letter.

Date Address

Greeting

Write about something bad that happened to you

Write about what has happened since then

Write about something good that happened to you

Closing

Sign your name

Exercise 5.3 Compose a friendly letter by filling in each of the following boxes with the suggested information. Put two or three sentences in each of the three boxes in the body of the letter.

Date Your address

Greeting

Write about the house or apartment where you live

Write about the neighborhood or town where you live

Write about the kind of house you would like to own someday

Closing

Sign your name

Exercise 5.4 Following the format shown in the first three exercises, write a friendly letter to a friend, a relative, or someone very close to you.

The Business Letter

There are some important differences between a friendly letter and a business letter. And although this second kind of letter is called a *business letter*, its style is used for any kind of formal letter. It is not used exclusively for conducting business.

Most businesses have *letterhead* paper. This is paper that already has the company logo, name, and address preprinted on it. At the top of the paper you will see something like this:

JONES AND SONS
Plumbing Done Right
2990 West Main Street
Johnstown, IL 60622
(311) 555-1234

Most individuals do not use letterhead, so the examples of business letters given here will be for paper without a letterhead.

There are several possible parts to a business letter. Compare these to the parts of a friendly letter:

- Start with the date on the left. Then include your return address, about two lines below the date. Your phone number is often included immediately following your address.

  June 30, 2003

  2990 West Main Street
  Johnstown, IL 60622
  (311) 555-1234

- Skip a line and then type the name of the person to whom you are writing followed by the company name and address.

  Ms. Mary Brown
  Jones Medical Center
  400 East Oak Street
  Johnstown, IL 60634

- If you don't know the name of the person to whom you should be writing, use an attention line to identify who should be looking at your letter (manager, accountant, etc.).

  Attention: Billing Manager

- Give the subject of the letter on its own line.
  Subject: Billing Problem

- The greeting is next, followed by a colon (:).
  Dear Ms. Brown:

- Skip a line and then begin the body of the letter. Use as many lines or paragraphs as necessary to express why you have written to this person.
  I am a patient who . . .

- Include a polite final statement on its own line, if you wish.
  Thank you.

- Close the letter and follow it with a comma.
  Sincerely,

- Skip four lines to provide a place to sign the letter.
  [Your signature]

- Type your full name and title (Manager, Chairperson, etc.) after the space left for your signature.
  [Your typed name]
  [Your title]

- If someone else typed your letter, show your initials in capital letters (WS), followed by a slash, followed by the initials of the person who typed the letter in lower case (bk).
  WS/bk

- If you are enclosing a document with your letter, skip a line and indicate that at the end of the letter.
  Enclosure (1)

If a business letter is typewritten, it should always be single-spaced. Let's look at some sample letters.

Sample 1 You know the name of the person to whom you are writing.

June 30, 2003

2990 West Main Street
Johnstown, IL 60622
(311) 555-1234

Ms. Mary Brown
Jones Medical Center
400 East Oak Street
Johnstown, IL 60634

Subject: Billing Problem

Dear Ms. Brown:

I am a patient who underwent outpatient surgery on my left hand on May 3, 2003. My doctor was Dr. Wilma Jones, and I am insured by the Johnstown HMO. My insurance number is ABC2003.

On June 25, 2003, I received a bill from your office in the amount of $2,500.00. It is my understanding that my insurer will cover $2,400.00 of this amount.

Please contact Mr. Roger Smith at Johnstown HMO for confirmation of my insurance and to adjust my bill. Inform me of any other steps I must take to correct this error.

I have enclosed a copy of my insurance policy with this letter.

Thank you.

Sincerely,

William Green
WG/bk

Enclosure (1)

Sample 2 You do not know the name of the person to whom you are writing.

June 30, 2003

2990 West Main Street
Johnstown, IL 60622
(311) 555-1234

Jones Medical Center
400 East Oak Street
Johnstown, IL 60634

Attention: Billing Manager

Subject: Billing Problem

I am a patient who underwent outpatient surgery on my left hand on May 3, 2003. My doctor was Dr. Wilma Jones, and I am insured by the Johnstown HMO. My insurance number is ABC2003.

On June 25, 2003, I received a bill from your office in the amount of $2,500.00. It is my understanding that my insurer will cover $2,400.00 of this amount.

Please contact Mr. Roger Smith at Johnstown HMO for confirmation of my insurance and to adjust my bill. Inform me of any other steps I must take to correct this error.

I have enclosed a copy of my insurance policy with this letter.

Thank you.

Sincerely,

William Green
WG/bk

Enclosure (1)

The Body of a Business Letter

The body (content) of a business or formal letter is very different from the body of a friendly letter. A business letter isn't casual, it isn't newsy, and it doesn't contain personal details that have nothing to do with the purpose of the letter. A business letter is *brief* and *to the point*. Look at how the body of the preceding sample business letters fits into the descriptions that follow:

- The first paragraph of a business letter introduces *you* and *the subject of the letter*. (I am a patient. I had hand surgery.)
- The second paragraph describes the *details* of the reason for the letter. (I received a bill for the surgery, but I have insurance. There's a mistake.)
- If there is a third paragraph, it provides *additional information* needed to understand the reason for the letter.
- The final paragraph *summarizes what you want to happen* and can contain a word of thanks. (Contact my insurance company. Let me know what else I have to do.)
- Describe any *enclosures* in the letter. (My insurance policy.)

Exercise 5.5 Compose a business letter by filling in each of the following boxes with the suggested information. Put two or three sentences in each of the three boxes in the body of the letter. You are complaining about a defective product.

Date

Your address

Name and address of the person you're writing to

Subject:

Greeting

Introduce yourself and the subject of the letter.

Give the details of the defective product.

Summarize what you want done.

A polite statement

Closing

Sign your name

Your name

Title (if any)

Enclosures (if any)

Exercise 5.6 Compose a business letter by filling in each of the following boxes with the suggested information. Put two or three sentences in each of the three boxes in the body of the letter. Inquire about job opportunities in a large business.

Date

Your address

Name and address of the person you're writing to

Subject:

Greeting

Introduce yourself and the subject of the letter.

Give the details of the reason for writing the letter.

Summarize what you want done.

A polite statement

Closing

Sign your name

Your name

Title (if any)

Enclosures (if any)

Exercise 5.7 Compose a business letter by filling in each of the following boxes with the suggested information. Put two or three sentences in each of the three boxes in the body of the letter. Complain about a poorly heated apartment and what you want done. You do not know the name of the person to whom you are writing.

Date

Your address

Address you're writing to

Attention:

Subject:

Introduce yourself and state your complaint.

Give the details of the complaint in a polite fashion.

Summarize what you want done.

A final statement

Closing

Sign your name

Your name

Title (if any)

Enclosures (if any)

Exercise 5.8 Write a business letter to a travel agency to get information about a trip you would like to take. You can get the address of a travel agency in the phone book.

Exercise 5.9 Write a business letter to a professional sports team to get its schedule of games for the next season. You can get the address of a sports team in the phone book.

6

Writing Original Themes

All the writing exercises you have done until now were the building blocks to get to this kind of writing: original themes. In this chapter you will create entire stories in your own words and using your own English skills. Don't be afraid to experiment or to try something unusual or fun. You should enjoy your writing.

With each exercise theme you will find suggestions for using certain grammatical structures or certain vocabulary. They are meant to guide you to writing a good theme. Naturally, you are the author of the themes and can add other kinds of structures and vocabulary and omit the suggested ones. You can decide what is most appropriate for your theme.

After you have written a theme, you can look at a sample theme of the same title in the Answer Key. That might give you some ideas for improving your theme.

Directions: Set a time limit for yourself of about thirty to fifty minutes. Try to use the same amount of time for each exercise. That will help you follow your progress more objectively. Look at the suggested structures and, if you wish, use them anywhere in your theme. You should write at least three paragraphs on each theme.

Exercise 6.1 *The Car I've Always Wanted*

Include these structures:

two comparatives and three superlatives (such as *bigger, biggest*)
one irregular verb in the past tense (example: "I saw the accident.")

Some helpful ideas for the theme:

What are the make, model, and color of the car?
How much does it cost, and how do you get the money?
Why do you need a car?
What happened to your last car?

Some helpful vocabulary words: *brakes, tires, car dealership, car loan, tune-up, convertible*

Exercise 6.2 *Death Came for a Visit*

Include these structures:

two possessive adjectives (such as *my, your, his, her*)

three relative pronouns (such as *that, who, which*)

Some helpful ideas for the theme:

Who was dying?

What happened to this person?

What is your relationship to this person?

How do you feel about death?

Some helpful vocabulary words: *illness, tragedy, sadness, comforting words, condolences*

Exercise 6.3 *The Most Unforgettable Day*

Include these structures:

two irregular verbs in the present perfect tense (example: "He has taken swimming lessons before.")

two reflexive pronouns (such as *myself, yourself, himself*)

one use of the preposition *because of*

Some helpful ideas for the theme:

Where were you on this day?

What happened?

Why was it so unforgettable?

Whom were you with?

Some helpful vocabulary words: *excitement, surprise, good fortune, amazing, happiness*

Exercise 6.4 *Peace or War*

Include these structures:

two passive voice verbs in the past tense (example: "She was found alive.")

three irregular verbs

Some helpful ideas for the theme:

What nations were in conflict?

Why was there the possibility of war?

Who wanted war and who wanted peace?

Is war always bad?

Some helpful vocabulary words: *army, military, negotiations, tension, attack, diplomacy*

Exercise 6.5 *A Wedding*

Include these structures:

two uses of the preposition *instead of*

two elliptical relative pronouns (example: "The man I spoke about is here.")

one future perfect tense verb (example: "He will have been found.")

Some helpful ideas for the theme:

Who was getting married?

Were the two families happy about the wedding?

Where did the wedding take place?

What was the celebration like?

Some helpful vocabulary words: *bride and groom, wedding ceremony, exchange of vows, in-laws, reception*

Exercise 6.6 *Credit Cards*

Include these structures:

two subjunctives following *if* (example: "If he were here, I would be happy.")

three compound sentences combined by *and*

Some helpful ideas for the theme:

Why does someone need a credit card?

How do you use a credit card?

Why are credit cards sometimes bad?

What happens if you can't pay your bills?

Some helpful vocabulary words: *ATM, shopping spree, emergencies, good (bad) credit, interest rate*

Exercise 6.7 *I Need a Vacation*

Include these structures:

three possessive nouns formed with *-'s* (example: "Bill's house")

two future tense phrases formed from *going to* (example: "I am going to buy that.")

Some helpful ideas for the theme:
What are some popular vacation spots?
Why does someone need a vacation?
What does a vacation cost?
What can you do on a vacation?
Who goes along?

Some helpful vocabulary words: *travel agent, airline, beach, hotels and motels, sightseeing, dinner and dancing*

Exercise 6.8 *The Person I Love Most*

Include these structures:
two statements following the conjunction *that* (example: "I know that you have my money.")
two relative clauses beginning with *that* (example: "Is she the girl that took the book?")
one use of the adjective *that* (example: "That man is a thief.")

Some helpful ideas for the theme:
Who is this loved person?
Why do you love him or her?
What is the difference between family love and romantic love?
How does this person feel about you?

Some helpful vocabulary words: *adore, respect, personality, companionship, soul mate, engagement*

Exercise 6.9 *If I Had a Million Dollars*

Include these structures:
two passive voice verbs in the present perfect tense (example: "It has been destroyed.")
three questions beginning with an interrogative word (such as *who, what, where*)

Some helpful ideas for the theme:
How would it feel to be rich?
What would you buy?
Whom would you help?
Are there problems with being rich?

Some helpful vocabulary words: *lottery, wealth, extravagance, mansion, limousine, charity*

Exercise 6.10 *My First Job*

Include these structures:

one use of the auxiliary *ought to* (example: "You ought to get a haircut.")

two uses of the auxiliary *have to* (example: "I have to go to work now.")

one use of the auxiliary *be able to* (example: "She was able to walk again.")

Some helpful ideas for the theme:

What kind of job were you looking for?
What kind of work did you do?
How much was the pay?
What was your boss like?
Why did that job end?

Some helpful vocabulary words: *manager, factory, clerk, paycheck, overtime, being fired, promotion*

Exercise 6.11 *Your Autobiography*

Make this final exercise creative and challenging by writing the story of your own life. You will likely use all of the structures mentioned previously and you should use a wide variety of vocabulary words.

Appendix

Irregular Verbs in the Past Tense and Past Participle

PRESENT TENSE	PAST TENSE	PAST PARTICIPLE
am, are, is	was, were	been
bear	bore	born, borne
beat	beat	beat, beaten
become	became	become
begin	began	begun
bend	bent	bent
bet	bet	bet
bind	bound	bound
bleed	bled	bled
blow	blew	blown
break	broke	broken
bring	brought	brought
build	built	built
burn	burned, burnt	burned, burnt
buy	bought	bought
can	could	—
catch	caught	caught
choose	chose	chosen
cost	cost	cost
creep	crept	crept
cut	cut	cut
dig	dug	dug
do	did	done
draw	drew	drawn
drink	drank	drunk
drive	drove	driven
eat	ate	eaten

PRESENT TENSE	PAST TENSE	PAST PARTICIPLE
fall	fell	fallen
feed	fed	fed
feel	felt	felt
fight	fought	fought
find	found	found
fly	flew	flown
forget	forgot	forgot, forgotten
freeze	froze	frozen
get	got	got, gotten
give	gave	given
go	went	gone
grow	grew	grown
hang	hung	hung
have, has	had	had
hear	heard	heard
hide	hid	hidden
hit	hit	hit
hold	held	held
hurt	hurt	hurt
keep	kept	kept
know	knew	known
lay	laid	laid
lead	led	led
leap	leaped, leapt	leaped, leapt
leave	left	left
let	let	let
lie	lay	lain
light	lit, lighted	lit, lighted
lose	lost	lost
make	made	made
may	might	—
mean	meant	meant
pay	paid	paid
put	put	put
read	read	read
ride	rode	ridden
ring	rang	rung
rise	rose	risen

PRESENT TENSE	PAST TENSE	PAST PARTICIPLE
run	ran	run
say	said	said
see	saw	seen
sell	sold	sold
send	sent	sent
shake	shook	shaken
shoot	shot	shot
show	showed	shown
shut	shut	shut
sing	sang	sung
sink	sank	sunk
sit	sat	sat
sleep	slept	slept
speak	spoke	spoken
speed	sped	sped
spend	spent	spent
spring	sprang	sprung
stand	stood	stood
steal	stole	stolen
stink	stank, stunk	stunk
swear	swore	sworn
swim	swam	swum
take	took	taken
teach	taught	taught
tear	tore	torn
tell	told	told
think	thought	thought
throw	threw	thrown
understand	understood	understood
wear	wore	worn
wed	wedded	wedded, wed
will	would	—
win	won	won
work	worked, wrought	worked, wrought
write	wrote	written

Answer Key

Exercise 1.1

1. Her brother looked for us. Her brother had looked for us. Her brother will look for us.
2. Are you looking for your wallet? Have you been looking for your wallet? Had you been looking for your wallet? Will you be looking for your wallet?
3. Does she help Tom? Did she help Tom? Has she helped Tom? Had she helped Tom?
4. I don't fill out the application. I didn't fill out the application. I hadn't filled out the application. I won't fill out the application.
5. Did they play soccer? Have they played soccer? Had they played soccer? Will they play soccer?
6. He is making a good salary. He was making a good salary. He has been making a good salary. He had been making a good salary.
7. Juan visits his aunt and uncle. Juan visited his aunt and uncle. Juan has visited his aunt and uncle. Juan will visit his aunt and uncle. Juan will have visited his aunt and uncle.
8. She carries the child to her bed. She has carried the child to her bed. She had carried the child to her bed. She will carry the child to her bed.
9. My sister often dated Michael. My sister has often dated Michael. My sister had often dated Michael. My sister will often date Michael.
10. They hire him. They hired him. They had hired him. They will hire him.

Exercise 1.2

1. Her brother was very rich. Her brother had been very rich. Her brother will be very rich.
2. Are the children good? Have the children been good? Had the children been good? Will the children be good?
3. Is she ill? Was she ill? Has she been ill? Had she been ill?

4. I am not angry at all. I was not angry at all. I had not been angry at all. I will not be angry at all.
5. Did you go there often? Have you gone there often? Had you gone there often? Will you go there often?
6. What do you do? What did you do? What have you done? What had you done?
7. The girls have a bad day. The girls had a bad day. The girls have had a bad day. The girls will have a bad day. The girls will have had a bad day.
8. Maria has ten dollars. Maria has had ten dollars. Maria had had ten dollars. Maria will have ten dollars.
9. My brother did nothing all day. My brother has done nothing all day. My brother had done nothing all day. My brother will do nothing all day.
10. They don't go to the movies. They didn't go to the movies. They hadn't gone to the movies. They won't go to the movies.

Exercise 1.3

1. Mark liked the new girl. Mark had liked the new girl. Mark will like the new girl.
2. Her boss was trying to understand. Her boss has been trying to understand. Her boss had been trying to understand. Her boss will be trying to understand.
3. The letter carriers go into the office. The letter carriers have gone into the office. The letter carriers had gone into the office. The letter carriers will go into the office. The letter carriers will have gone into the office.
4. Are you talking to Richard? Have you been talking to Richard? Had you been talking to Richard? Will you be talking to Richard?
5. His son breaks a window. His son broke a window. His son had broken a window. His son will break a window.
6. The secretary is writing letters. The secretary was writing letters. The secretary had been writing letters. The secretary will be writing letters.
7. Don't you sing, too? Didn't you sing, too? Haven't you sung, too? Hadn't you sung, too?
8. They aren't going shopping. They weren't going shopping. They haven't been going shopping. They hadn't been going shopping.
9. Carlos gets up before dawn. Carlos got up before dawn. Carlos has gotten up before dawn. Carlos had gotten up before dawn. Carlos will get up before dawn.

10. By seven-thirty he leaves for home. By seven-thirty he left for home. By seven-thirty he has left for home. By seven-thirty he had left for home. By seven-thirty he will leave for home.

Exercise 1.4 Note that these are example answers. Your pronouns may differ.

1. Was he on time? Have I been on time? Had she been on time? Will they be on time?
2. Doesn't he like the book? Hadn't you liked the book? Won't they like the book?
3. We are driving very slowly. You were driving very slowly. They had been driving very slowly. She will be driving very slowly.
4. I find him just in time. You found him just in time. She has found him just in time. They will find him just in time. He will have found him just in time.
5. I arrange a party for her. You arranged a party for her. He has arranged a party for her. She had arranged a party for her. We will have arranged a party for her.
6. She brings it home by noon. I brought it home by noon. You have brought it home by noon. They had brought it home by noon. We will bring it home by noon.
7. I ate too much. He has eaten too much. She had eaten too much. We will eat too much.
8. You put the tools back before lunch. He has put the tools back before lunch. She had put the tools back before lunch. We will put the tools back before lunch. They will have put the tools back before lunch.
9. I cut out the dress before bedtime. You have cut out the dress before bedtime. He had cut out the dress before bedtime. We will cut out the dress before bedtime. They will have cut out the dress before bedtime.
10. I steal the money by midnight. You stole the money by midnight. They had stolen the money by midnight. She will steal the money by midnight.

Exercise 1.5

1. Are they going to bring some dessert along?
2. I'm going to be home at midnight.
3. The janitor is going to sweep the offices after closing time.
4. He isn't going to return the money he borrowed.

5. This movie is going to be very exciting.
6. The party is going to be held at Maria's house.
7. Is Martin going to apply for a new job?
8. She is probably going to spend the night at Mary's apartment.
9. Are you going to order a hamburger or a hot dog?
10. The boys are going to clean the kitchen for you.

Exercise 1.6

1. Could you hear me well enough? (Were you able to hear me well enough?) Have you been able to hear me well enough? Had you been able to hear me well enough? Will you be able to hear me well enough?
2. Martin wants to buy a car. Martin has wanted to buy a car. Martin had wanted to buy a car. Martin will want to buy a car.
3. I am supposed to go home by eight o'clock. I had been supposed to go home by eight o'clock.
4. Might I try on your new coat?
5. She was not able to visit you today. She has not been able to visit you today. She had not been able to visit you today. She will not be able to visit you today.
6. Do you have to study before the test? Did you have to study before the test? Had you had to study before the test? Will you have to study before the test? Will you have had to study before the test?
7. one tense = shouldn't
8. one tense = ought to
9. Juan had to work all day. Juan has had to work all day. Juan had had to work all day. Juan will have to work all day. Juan will have had to work all day.
10. She doesn't need to get there on time. She didn't need to get there on time. She hasn't needed to get there on time. She won't need to get there on time.

Exercise 1.7

1. James wants to borrow a book from Maria.
2. I needed to find some extra money.
3. Mr. Sanchez must leave his luggage at the door.
4. Could you already speak English as a child?
5. We haven't been able to write the whole assignment.
6. You were supposed to help me.

7. The children ought to be careful.
8. Why should they live in that little apartment?
9. I have often wanted to travel to Europe.
10. Nick may read all the books on the top shelf.
11. We will have to take the train as far as Chicago.
12. They were able to speak with very little accent.
13. Can you help the child tie his shoes?
14. The designers are supposed to turn their work in on time.
15. Will Victor have to work overtime tomorrow?

Exercise 1.8

1. We don't go to the movies.
2. He doesn't eat so fast.
3. After supper we took a little nap.
4. Tomorrow I'll go shopping for a new hat.
5. Why do you always lie to me?
6. Theresa hasn't helped her grandmother this week.
7. The guests leave their coats at the door.
8. Vera got everyone a little gift.
9. If you contact me after nine o'clock, call this number.
10. At what time do we go for lunch?
11. The tourists go to the museum early.
12. Juanita goes out on a date with Richard.
13. This is enough.
14. I see the Grand Canyon.
15. My nephew didn't repair his car yet.

Exercise 1.9 Sample answers are provided.

1. must
2. can
3. must
4. wants to
5. need to
6. are supposed to
7. should
8. can
9. has to
10. want to

11. should
12. May
13. may
14. must
15. wanted to

Exercise 1.10 Sample phrases are provided.

1. eat so much
2. come home
3. to get out of bed
4. borrow your car
5. help out
6. to go right home
7. to buy her a gift
8. travel to Mexico
9. take some time off from work
10. have the next dance
11. swear so much
12. find time for you
13. relax more
14. fire her
15. drink so much

Exercise 1.11

1. Is the window repaired? Has the window been repaired? Had the window been repaired? Will the window be repaired? Will the window have been repaired?
2. The dog is struck by a car. The dog has been struck by a car. The dog had been struck by a car. The dog will be struck by a car. The dog will have been struck by a car.
3. The package is shipped by rail. The package was shipped by rail. The package had been shipped by rail. The package will be shipped by rail. The package will have been shipped by rail.
4. Everything is arranged. Everything was arranged. Everything had been arranged. Everything will be arranged. Everything will have been arranged.

5. The fort is attacked at dawn. The fort was attacked at dawn. The fort has been attacked at dawn. The fort will be attacked at dawn. The fort will have been attacked at dawn.
6. Her driver's license is taken away. Her driver's license was taken away. Her driver's license has been taken away. Her driver's license will be taken away. Her driver's license will have been taken away.
7. A new song is written for the rock concert. A new song was written for the rock concert. A new song has been written for the rock concert. A new song had been written for the rock concert. A new song will have been written for the rock concert.
8. Is the injured man rescued in time? Was the injured man rescued in time? Has the injured man been rescued in time? Had the injured man been rescued in time? Will the injured man have been rescued in time?
9. Isn't the damage noticed by then? Wasn't the damage noticed by then? Hasn't the damage been noticed by then? Hadn't the damage been noticed by then? Won't the damage be noticed by then?
10. The king was whisked away to safety. The king has been whisked away to safety. The king had been whisked away to safety. The king will be whisked away to safety. The king will have been whisked away to safety.

Exercise 1.12

1. being
2. attacked
3. was
4. been
5. be
6. changed
7. spoken
8. wasn't
9. blown
10. been
11. has not
12. declared
13. be
14. being
15. is

Exercise 1.13

1. speak
2. sing
3. find
4. be
5. had
6. would be
7. played . . . would win
8. would have bought . . . had been
9. were
10. hire
11. had seen . . . would have reported
12. live
13. would speak . . . smiled
14. would have helped . . . had known
15. be

Exercise 1.14

1. If Jorge had been at home, he would have answered the telephone.
2. If you had earned enough money, you would have been able to buy the car.
3. If Alicia had sent him a picture, he would have been the happiest man alive.
4. I wouldn't have said such a thing if I had been the boss.
5. My brother would have sold the old radio if it had been his.
6. Would you really have kissed me if I had asked you to?
7. If Mr. Johnson had gotten a ticket, his wife would have been very angry with him.
8. If it had snowed, they would have had to go skiing.
9. If Robert had overslept again, he would have lost his job.
10. If only my sister had been here.
11. Would you have trusted me again if I had given you my word of honor?
12. I wouldn't have liked it at all if Barbara had gone out with Bill.
13. If the carpenter had had time, he would have built you a nice cabinet.
14. If he had known the truth, he wouldn't have written such a nasty letter.
15. If Enrique had worked harder, he wouldn't have needed to work overtime.

Exercise 1.15

1. If only he saw the truck in time.
2. I wouldn't give her the money if I knew why she wanted it.
3. Would you care if I went out on a date with Carmen?
4. Maria would have to stay overnight if she missed the last train.
5. If I didn't have a flat tire, I wouldn't miss the sale.
6. If only you were able to (could) forgive me.
7. The boss would fire her if he saw her sleeping on the job.
8. If he needed to borrow some money, he would come to me.
9. The thief would be caught if the police arrived sooner.
10. If the computer were repaired, the data files would be finished on time.

Exercise 1.16 Sample phrases are provided.

1. she would have said hello
2. you would lend me the money
3. were here
4. you showed me the way there
5. you had been nicer to him
6. you had more time
7. John weren't so lazy
8. Maria had been in town
9. you would have been able to buy the car
10. they won the lottery

Exercise 1.17

1. We went to bed early because it was such a tiring day.
2. Can you tell me where John is working?
3. Monday is the first day of classes, and I still have to buy some books.
4. Juan is my only brother, but I haven't seen him in a year.
5. The weather is terrible today; however, the parade went on as planned.
6. She started crying when I told her I love her.
7. I don't understand how you can live in the city.
8. The soldiers let out a cheer, for the war had finally ended.
9. Tom will help you if you pay him a few dollars.
10. We didn't know where she was hiding.
11. Let me know when you will be home.

12. It's been a long time since I last saw you.
13. Do your very best, but be careful.
14. She suddenly understood where Father got the money.
15. It's difficult to understand why we should help you.

Exercise 1.18 Sample phrases are provided.

1. played till dusk
2. I still enjoy living here
3. he hates working with numbers
4. going to work today was out of the question
5. the storm appeared to be getting worse
6. I suggest we stop the project
7. I'll continue to try to raise the money
8. we promise to pay him back soon
9. the dinosaurs became extinct
10. the problem is
11. he ever became our mayor
12. the fight started
13. the lights went out
14. the treasure was buried
15. the blizzard continues
16. it's still hard to trust you
17. we all can go home
18. the man pulled a gun from his shirt
19. you get a promotion
20. I'll get paid

Exercise 1.19 Sample phrases are provided.

1. The bear stopped and looked at me
2. I cared for it every day
3. Jim waited two hours at the door
4. She hid under an awning
5. He bought them dinner
6. There were no buses running
7. I often listen to jazz
8. they can begin their own business
9. No one understands

10. I don't think you know
11. I don't have any idea
12. The report suggested
13. there was a long line at the front door
14. I laughed out loud
15. Please tell me

Exercise 1.20

1. *He* stood up slowly and looked at the jury.
2. When I saw *them* on the corner, I gave a little wave.
3. I knew that *she* was our new boss.
4. Dr. Brown often wrote about *it* in her diary.
5. *They* were really much worse than mine.
6. I truly liked *his* daughter a lot.
7. *We* hoped to buy a car together.
8. I'd help if *her* brother would help.
9. I think that the last two chairs at the table are *ours*.
10. You ought to have a few words with *him*.

Exercise 1.21

1. *Their* bedroom needs to be painted.
2. Have you met *his* relatives?
3. It looks like *its* trunk is scratched.
4. Why is *its* cover torn off?
5. Her aunt is a physician in one of *its* clinics.
6. *His* neighbor used to work as a gardener.
7. *Her* voice began to crack.
8. Was *her* husband a carpenter, too?
9. *It* is really too small for their family.
10. I'd like to see *their* new house sometime.

Exercise 1.22

1. ourselves
2. him
3. myself
4. her, herself

5. them
6. himself
7. yourselves
8. itself
9. themselves
10. them
11. her
12. him, himself
13. it
14. yourself
15. ourselves

Exercise 1.23 Sample answers are provided.

1. a. I live in Boston. b. The girls like me. c. This is my new car.
2. a. You have a nice smile. b. She spoke with you. c. Is this your house?
3. a. She came from India. b. Where did you see her? c. Her family is large.
4. a. We need some cash. b. He did it for us. c. This is our new puppy.
5. a. They belong in a safe. b. Where did you buy them? c. Their nephew is a cadet.
6. a. It sat on the fence. b. Did you see it? c. Its eyes were blood red.
7. a. He lived in Mexico. b. Do you know him? c. This is his father.

Exercise 1.24

1. We decided to buy the newspaper that was printed in London.
2. Helena caught a fish that was nearly two feet long.
3. Are you going to rent the apartment in which William lived?
4. I have often chatted with the policeman that my father knows.
5. There was a horrible storm, which destroyed many trees.
6. We're going to the beach that my grandparents live near.
7. May I have the bike that is in need of repair?
8. They all like the new boss, who got them pay raises.
9. David's mother is in the hospital, which is located on Main Street.
10. Do you have the money that I put on this table?
11. The children were lost in the forest in which an ugly witch lived.
12. I don't understand the problem that you wrote about in your letter.
13. Several men found the bear whose cubs had died.

14. She shouldn't wear the dress that has a stain on it.
15. They captured the officer whose troops attacked the fort.

Exercise 1.25

1. She agreed to buy the car I saw in the city.
2. Do you have the money I lent you?
3. Where's the lamp I put on this table?
4. That's the fellow I got the tickets from.
5. Tom got a job in the factory my father works in.
6. Where did you find the books I lost?
7. Juan wrote the poem Maria is reading right now.
8. Help me find the kitten the dog chased into the garden.
9. There's the airline pilot we visited last week.
10. The thief stole the camera I had placed on this bench a moment ago.
11. This is the heroic boy the reporter wrote about.
12. I was the one who bought the bottle of beer Robert drank.
13. Our boss fired the girl he had argued with.
14. Carmen lived in the same town I lived in years ago.
15. Why did you break the window Dad just repaired?

Exercise 1.26 Sample phrases are provided.

1. was famous for its beauty
2. I learned so much about America
3. just jumped that fence
4. he admires very much
5. he wrote in his youth
6. blocks the road to California
7. they made in England
8. is easier to use
9. jokes are so funny
10. you got your change
11. Tom told us about
12. must have cost a fortune
13. she wrote about in her letters
14. cannot be resolved easily
15. he gave her on their anniversary

Exercise 1.27

1. I helped the young student, whose grades were terrible.
2. Where's the fellow whose car won't start?
3. I bought an old car, the interior of which was in bad condition.
4. Where's the woman whose husband still lives in Mexico?
5. I need a carton, the size of which has to be two feet by three feet by three feet.
6. Juan discovered a cave, the ceiling of which was more than thirty feet high.
7. The doctor examined the child whose temperature was over one hundred degrees.
8. The teacher punished the boys whose behavior was awful.
9. He reread the words, the meaning of which was beyond his understanding.
10. Juanita tasted the cake, the flavor of which was wonderful.

Exercise 1.28

1. The young man's
2. of her eyes
3. the jury's
4. the captain's
5. The women's
6. of his words
7. Our teams'
8. our team's
9. of these countries
10. Thomas'

Exercise 1.29

1. *The geese* had laid *golden eggs*.
2. *My uncles* bought *the houses* at the edge of town.
3. *The churches* were damaged by *the storms*.
4. *Soldiers* carried *the helpless infants* to safety.
5. Did *the women* find *their children*?
6. *Strange men* came up to *the windows* and looked in.
7. *Their bosses* are going to fire *the new employees*.

8. *Large boards* fell on Juan and broke *his feet*.
9. *The cities* are too far from *the factories*.
10. *The nurses* covered *the patients* with *heavy blankets*.

Exercise 1.30

1. The boys'
2. the animals
3. your parents'
4. the men's
5. Mr. Roberts'
6. of names
7. the airports
8. a grown woman
9. of soup
10. eggs
11. the boss'
12. The tourist's
13. my brother's
14. his stories
15. Tom's feet

Exercise 1.31

1. My sister is prettier than my cousin.
2. Our team played poorer (or more poorly) than your team.
3. Uncle William was richer than Uncle James.
4. Raquel can run faster than her brother.
5. The roses are more delicate than the daisies.
6. Thomas really works better than anyone else.
7. Finding a job is more important than watching TV.
8. He wrote his signature more rapidly than the address.
9. Ms. Johnson is friendlier than Mr. Johnson.
10. Can you speak louder (or more loudly) than James?
11. Tom is more responsible than his sister.
12. A fox is slier than a rabbit.
13. My nephew knows more funny stories than my niece.
14. The bees are busier than the ants.
15. He knows less about math than about history.

Exercise 1.32

1. My sister is the prettiest.
2. The best recipes are in this book.
3. Your nephew does the least work around the house.
4. The most important idea in the book is learning to be patient.
5. Maria swam fastest and won a blue ribbon.
6. I have the most problems.
7. I feel that Juan is the most intelligent one.
8. Bill arrived the earliest and left the latest.
9. The oldest car costs the least money.
10. Your pronunciation is the worst.
11. I think yours is the best idea.
12. An SUV is the most logical choice for a family car.
13. My aunt has the most money.
14. Alicia spoke the most brilliantly about the Civil War.
15. This brown pup is the smallest.

Exercise 2.1

1. isn't difficult
2. whose machine
3. him
4. back down
5. several tiny kittens
6. if
7. During
8. was more embarrassed
9. rather doubtful
10. several issues
11. find
12. relates to me
13. won't stand
14. the richest man
15. how
16. regarding
17. the color of which
18. been
19. therefore
20. themselves

Exercise 2.2 Sample answers are provided.

1. will
2. the weather got better
3. we're still in town
4. been
5. to
6. will
7. worried
8. which
9. ought to
10. has
11. because
12. playing
13. will
14. may
15. was
16. to
17. able
18. that
19. that
20. I've come down with a cold

Exercise 2.3 Sample answers are provided.

1. By noon tomorrow
2. When
3. The technician
4. had been
5. transferred
6. how the climate changes
7. I'm free the following day
8. sign the contract
9. to be out so late
10. won't
11. hadn't
12. speaks English . . . only speaks Spanish
13. to get
14. phone you . . . phone me
15. you better . . . probably believe more of what you say

16. you in the window . . . were the girl for me
17. approach her . . . even look at him
18. tell me . . . is located
19. you had to hear the news from me
20. he had been dreaming about
21. the woman
22. understand how I feel
23. I'm leaving town
24. mind my own business
25. write you . . . you were still dating Juan

Exercise 2.4 Sample answers are provided.

1. I fell into bed exhausted
2. Do you have any idea
3. I've been here two months
4. we can't seem to get along
5. Go hiking in the mountains
6. she's a rock musician herself
7. a trip to the zoo sounded good
8. they lost their jobs in the city
9. you have to pay for dinner
10. she was speaking
11. this firm won't hire me
12. your story is unbelievable
13. we can finally continue the hike
14. the car stalled in the middle of the street
15. the streets are still flooded
16. you get a promotion
17. I got fired
18. you'd help me locate my parents
19. you hadn't brought up the subject
20. You wouldn't have been in debt

Exercise 2.5 Sample answers are provided.

1. The door flew open
2. He tried everything
3. We were late for the interview

4. We had to rebuild it
5. I was staring into the distance
6. Does anyone know
7. Maria and Juan began to get nervous
8. You'll go broke
9. he had known about the transmission
10. he had had the down payment
11. be a bit more polite
12. my vacation
13. Many old people got ill
14. plane had been shot down
15. you find a new place to work
16. be a bother to you
17. the bride . . . the groom
18. the doctor . . . his office hours begin
19. ever loved
20. I'm going to be forty soon

Exercise 3.1 Sample sentences are provided.

1. The new waiter works hard.
2. Have you seen the new waiter?
3. I sent the new waiter a note.
4. I have a message for the new waiter.
5. Friends of the new waiter are at the door.
6. The new waiter has broken every rule.
7. The new waiter soon will have earned enough for his vacation.
8. The new waiter quit, and the cook went wild.
9. Where's the new waiter that you hired?
10. This is the new waiter I spoke of.

Exercise 3.2 Sample sentences are provided.

1. Some old friends came for a visit.
2. I found some old friends.
3. I gave the book to some old friends.
4. It was taken by some old friends.
5. He has met some old friends' relatives.
6. Some old friends came up to me.

7. I went out with her because some old friends introduced us.
8. Come meet some old friends who just got in from Chicago.
9. Some old friends were approached by a strange man.
10. If she had loved me, some old friends would have told me so.

Exercise 3.3 Sample sentences are provided.

1. The new boss is nice.
2. Tom wrote the new boss a memo.
3. I quit because the new boss is so rude.
4. This is a package for the new boss.
5. I got this memo from the new boss.
6. The new boss has a large office, and I have a cubicle.
7. She was happy because the new boss gave her a raise.
8. The new boss has been shocked into reality by the job.
9. The new boss was being tested his first few days.
10. If you had helped us, the new boss wouldn't have gotten so mad.

Exercise 3.4 Sample sentences are provided.

1. Two dangerous criminals escaped.
2. They began an investigation into two dangerous criminals.
3. They locked the doors because of two dangerous criminals.
4. He discovered two dangerous criminals' fingerprints.
5. When I saw him, two dangerous criminals were talking to him.
6. Two dangerous criminals have been sneaking around the park.
7. I'm afraid because two dangerous criminals threatened me.
8. They're looking for two dangerous criminals who escaped last week.
9. Two dangerous criminals have been transferred to this prison.
10. If we had the money, two dangerous criminals would soon come after us.

Exercise 3.5 Sample sentences are provided.

1. Our Mexican guests are from Acapulco.
2. She liked our Mexican guests.
3. What should we send our Mexican guests?
4. Tom went up to our Mexican guests.
5. The gift was sent by our Mexican guests.
6. He invited them instead of our Mexican guests.

7. Our Mexican guests have driven from Juarez.
8. Our Mexican guests will have arrived here by dawn.
9. Say hello to our Mexican guests, who just arrived today.
10. Bill met our Mexican guests we had invited to visit us last year.

Exercise 3.6 Sample sentences are provided.

1. The bravest woman received a medal.
2. He came toward the bravest woman with a sword in his hand.
3. We stood by the bravest woman.
4. The bravest woman has shown who is the strongest.
5. I met the bravest woman, who had led the village in the battle.
6. I saw the bravest woman that everyone admired so much.
7. Tom photographed the bravest woman he had ever met.
8. The bravest woman has been showered with gifts.
9. The bravest woman was congratulated for her deeds.
10. If he had lived longer, he would have thanked the bravest woman for her kindness.

Exercise 3.7 Sample sentences are provided.

1. Do you have a registered letter?
2. Did the package come without a registered letter?
3. He made the decision in spite of a registered letter on his desk.
4. I don't want to know the contents of a registered letter.
5. A registered letter has been missing for some time.
6. A registered letter will have shown up for you before noon.
7. A telegram came for me, and a registered letter came for you.
8. I'm always nervous because a registered letter means someone has died.
9. I found a registered letter, which is addressed to you.
10. She was reading a registered letter that had come in the day before.

Exercise 3.8 Sample sentences are provided.

1. What did you buy the proud parents?
2. Everyone was happy because of the proud parents.
3. The children waited eagerly because the proud parents would be home soon.
4. The proud parents have been hoping for a son.

5. The proud parents will have left the hospital by ten a.m.
6. She wanted to see the new baby, and the proud parents slowly raised the blanket.
7. They all laughed because the proud parents couldn't smile anymore.
8. The proud parents have been congratulated over and over.
9. The proud parents were led into a separate room.
10. If it had snowed, the proud parents would have celebrated at the hospital.

Exercise 3.9 Sample sentences are provided.

1. His youngest daughter is in law school.
2. He bought his youngest daughter a car.
3. They turned down his youngest daughter.
4. His youngest daughter drove to New Orleans.
5. When I saw him, his youngest daughter was chatting with him.
6. His youngest daughter will have arrived by now.
7. He was worried because his youngest daughter was in an accident.
8. I met his youngest daughter, who shared an apartment with Anna.
9. His youngest daughter has been sent overseas.
10. If I had been wrong, his youngest daughter would have told me so.

Exercise 3.10 Sample sentences are provided.

1. There's no talking to an angry mob.
2. He feared going out because of an angry mob.
3. You'll get no justice from an angry mob.
4. An angry mob's demands went unheard.
5. An angry mob has held them at bay.
6. An angry mob has been hunting down the strikebreakers.
7. An angry mob began to move, and the police became jittery.
8. I know nothing about an angry mob.
9. You can't stop an angry mob sent with the blessings of the dictator.
10. An angry mob was formed from several groups of jobless men.

Exercise 3.11 Sample sentences are provided.

1. Several pretty girls entered the contest.
2. I sent several pretty girls flowers.
3. I stayed at the beach because several pretty girls were nearby.

4. The man moved toward several pretty girls.
5. Several pretty girls sold kisses for charity.
6. Several pretty girls have become doctors and lawyers.
7. When I met him, he was in the company of several pretty girls.
8. Tom was happy because several pretty girls had complimented him.
9. Several pretty girls he knew were now studying acting.
10. If he had seen her, he wouldn't have spent so much time with several pretty girls.

Exercise 3.12 Sample sentences are provided.

1. The officer gave the drunken soldier a ticket.
2. There were lots of rowdy people there besides the drunken soldier.
3. She left the party because the drunken soldier was so rude.
4. No one wants to be around the drunken soldier.
5. The manners of the drunken soldier were terrible.
6. The drunken soldier has left the bar.
7. The drunken soldier has been drinking all night.
8. The drunken soldier finally went home because the café closed.
9. The drunken soldier has been taken into custody.
10. If it had rained, the drunken soldier wouldn't have noticed.

Exercise 3.13 Sample sentences are provided.

1. There was some writing on his driver's license.
2. He got a ticket because his driver's license wasn't valid.
3. What information did you get from his driver's license?
4. His driver's license has fallen behind a chair.
5. His driver's license has been lying on the floor all this time.
6. His passport is in the drawer, and his driver's license is in his wallet.
7. He went to the courthouse because his driver's license has to be renewed.
8. He handed me his driver's license, which was covered in blood.
9. His driver's license is being restored.
10. If she had seen us, he would have hidden his driver's license.

Exercise 3.14 Sample sentences are provided.

1. The best candidates have no money.
2. I trust the best candidates.
3. She lent the best candidates thousands of dollars.

4. In spite of the best candidates in the party, he supported Tom Jones.
5. The best candidates' platforms are based on honesty.
6. The best candidates understood our concerns.
7. The best candidates have flown from city to city during the campaign.
8. When I found them, the best candidates were huddled in a meeting.
9. The best candidates have been campaigning for weeks.
10. The best candidates will have met with thousands of people by then.

Exercise 3.15 Sample sentences are provided.

1. Do you know the bride and groom?
2. The bride and groom's happiness was evident.
3. The bride and groom stood hand in hand.
4. The bride and groom have spoken their vows.
5. When he hit me, the bride and groom rushed to my side.
6. The bride and groom, whose hometown is St. Louis, recently graduated from college.
7. The bride and groom that you met are from a different wedding party.
8. Say hello to the bride and groom I told you about.
9. The bride and groom have been asked to dance the first waltz.
10. If you had lied to me, the bride and groom would have been victims, too.

Exercise 4.1 Sample answers are provided.

Travel Plans

John and Mary wanted to take a vacation. They had worked hard all year and **had saved every extra penny**. But where should they go? To **someplace warm** or to **a place with interesting sightseeing**?

"I want to go to Mexico," Mary said. "I heard it's **beautiful there** and **the food is so interesting.**"

"I think I'd like to go to India," John replied. "I want to see **the great palaces** and **wild tigers and elephants**."

"India is so far away," Mary said to him. "I think **we should stay in North America**. Or we could travel to **Europe if you want to go somewhere a little more exotic**."

"Or how about **Hawaii**?" John said.

But no matter how much they talked, they couldn't **agree on a destination**. John believed **being in a large city was important**, but Mary wanted **to be in the countryside or at a beach**. How could they decide what would be best for both of them?

John opened the newspaper and saw **an ad for a resort outside of Miami**. He showed Mary the article, and she **thought the place looked inviting**.

"That sounds like fun," Mary said. "I'd love **to spend time at that pool or on the beach**."

"We could swim during the day, and at night **we could go dancing** or **dine in the city**," John said. "And we could go shopping **if the weather got bad**."

Mary was happy with the idea, because **the beach really appealed to her** and **she knew John would like visiting Miami**. John wouldn't mind spending time at the beach, because he knew **that it would make his wife so happy**. But there still was a problem.

"**Do we have enough money for such an expensive resort**?" Mary suddenly asked. "Do we have enough in the bank?"

John thought a moment, and then he **smiled slyly at Mary**. He opened the desk drawer and **pulled out a small book**. He showed Mary **a bank book with some extra money he had saved**, but she **was still concerned that a fancy resort was too expensive**. John smiled at her and said, "Don't worry. **This extra money should be enough**. And if it's not enough, we can **borrow a little more from the bank**."

"Oh, John," Mary said happily. "Now **we can have what we both want**. This vacation **will be the best one we ever had**."

Then he kissed her cheek, because **seeing his wife happy was the best part of any vacation.**

Exercise 4.2 Sample answers are provided.

The Ant and the Grasshopper

It was a beautiful summer day. The sky **was blue and dotted with white clouds**, and the field was filled with **swaying grass and pretty flowers**. A happy, green grasshopper with long legs and **twitching antennae** jumped from a bouncy leaf to **a slanting twig** and **sang a song as he looked around**. He was enjoying the wonderful weather. He sang to himself, as he **took in his beautiful surroundings.**

Then he saw a small black ant near **a dead tree limb**. She was pulling a crust of bread through **the dried leaves.** She tugged and pulled, but **her efforts never seemed quite enough**. Then the ant stopped for a moment to rest and **laid the crust of bread on the ground next to her**. "Why are you doing that?" the grasshopper asked. "**Are you going to waste this wonderful day on such foolishness?**" he inquired with a laugh.

"I'm bringing food to our colony," the little ant replied. "When winter comes, **this crust of bread will come in handy**."

"Winter is a long way off," the grasshopper said. "I'd rather **sing and relax in the sun**."

"You might be sorry when **it turns cold and the sun is behind the clouds**," the ant warned. "You should plan for **your future**."

But the grasshopper just laughed and **stretched his long legs**. He jumped over **a tin can** and hopped across **the long grasses**, playing, singing, and **being as lazy as a grasshopper can be**.

The little ant shook her head and went back to work. She **put the crust of bread on her back** and finally **got past the dead leaves and scurried home**.

The grasshopper saw the ant working nearly every day. And every day he just **watched with amusement**. Soon it began to grow cold. The wind **changed to the north and brought more cold with it**. The snow **began to fall and soon covered the fields where the grasshopper played**. And the grasshopper understood **that the ant had been right all along**. He made his way to the ant colony and called out, "**I need some food and shelter**." But the ants could not hear him. They **were busy feasting**, and the poor grasshopper **jumped from icy twig to icy leaf in search of food and some shelter from the cold**.

Exercise 4.3 Sample answers are provided.

I'm No Cook!

My wife was called away to New York on business. I took some vacation time and **decided I would take care of the house and our kids**. Our two kids were in school during the day, and **in the evening they stayed home to do homework or watch TV**. They were old enough to take care of themselves, but I had to **make their meals and wash their clothes**. John was eleven and spent his time **on his computer**. Anne was ten and enjoyed sports like **baseball and soccer**.

Everything started out smoothly the first day. I cleaned the kitchen and **scoured the bathtub and sinks**. I ironed **a stack of clean laundry** and took the dog **to the vet for a shot**. And for lunch I made myself **a meatball sandwich with a tall glass of beer**. The kids ate lunch **in the school cafeteria**, because **students weren't allowed to come home for lunch**.

At four o'clock I realized that the kids **would be on their way home**, so I decided to **get their supper ready**. I got a recipe book from the shelf and found **what looked like a simple plan for supper**. It seemed easy enough, although **there were three parts to the meal**. I got the ingredients I needed out of the cupboard: **flour, spices, oil, and vinegar**.

I started with the salad. I rinsed a head of lettuce and then **chopped it into large wedges**. I sliced **tomatoes and green peppers** and scattered them over the lettuce. But I forgot to **add the fresh cilantro**. I peeled a cucumber and an onion and **added them to the bowl of salad**. I sprinkled **some oil and vinegar** over the salad and went to place it in the refrigerator. But when I placed the bowl on the shelf in the refrigerator, the shelf broke and **the bowl fell and shattered, and salad went everywhere.**

I couldn't believe my eyes. There were **lettuce and tomatoes** on the floor and **green peppers and cucumbers** on my shoes. I grabbed a broom and **swept up most of it**. Then I got a bucket and scrub brush in order to **clean the floor and refrigerator**. When I was done, I sat down and **rested up from the ordeal**.

The roast looked easier to prepare. I placed it in a large pan and covered it **with flour and spices**. I sprinkled salt and pepper **over the whole roast** and **placed pieces of garlic across the top**. I peeled three potatoes and six **large carrots** and **placed them around the roast**. Before I put the roast in the oven, I checked the shelf. I didn't want **another accident to happen**. Then I carefully put the roast in the oven and **checked the shelf one more time.**

For dessert I made vanilla ice cream with **chocolate sauce and nuts**. That was Anne's favorite, and John **would eat anything that was sweet**. I put the three bowls of dessert on the counter. About four-thirty **I heard my son and daughter come in**. They went to their rooms to **start their homework**.

I set the table and then called **them down to supper**. They hurried into the kitchen and took their seats. John was hungry, and Anne **sniffed the air trying to figure out what was on the menu.** But something had gone wrong. I hadn't put the dessert in the refrigerator, and **the ice cream had melted**! And I had forgotten to turn on the oven, so the roast **was just a piece of raw flesh**!

The kids looked sad and **began to complain that they were hungry**. So we got in the car, and I took them **to a little Mexican café down the street**. We all love tacos and fajitas.

Exercise 4.4 Sample answers are provided.

The Circle of Stones

This was the strangest case the judge had ever had. A child had been lost for **six years** and **had been raised by peasants**. The poor child did not know its real mother, because **it had been an infant when it was lost**. Two women claimed to be the real mother and demanded **the right to take the child home**. The judge needed more information first and **decided to interrogate the two women**.

The first woman told of **a terrible flood in her village**, when **people were running for their lives and children were separated from their parents**. The judge understood but asked, "**Why didn't you return after the flood to look**

for the child?" The first woman just shook her head and **said that she believed the child had died**. Now the second woman gave her story, which **told of bandits who stole her cart, in which her baby had been sleeping**. She explained that **she looked for the bandits and her child for weeks, but they had disappeared into the countryside**, and the judge believed her. But who is the real mother? the judge thought. He looked at the child and asked, "**Do you know which of these women is your mother**?" But the sobbing child could only reply, "**I don't remember my mother**."

"Then we shall have a test," the judge said **with a clever look on his face**. He placed the child in a ring of stones and told the two women **to stand on either side of the child**. Each took the child by one hand, and **they were told to pull the child out of the ring of stones**. They pulled to the right and then **to the left**, and the child began **to move one way and then the other**.

The women pulled again, but **once more the child did not leave the ring of stones**. Finally the first woman saw her chance and **pulled as hard as she could**. The child fell forward and **rolled out of the ring of stones**. The first woman laughed and proclaimed, "**I have won, and the child is mine**." The second woman began to sob, because **she couldn't bear to hurt the child anymore**. And the child sat on the ground, shaking and **looking anxiously at the first woman**.

The judge stood up and said, "**No, the second woman is the winner**, because the second woman would not harm the child. Therefore I am certain that **she is the real mother**."

He gave the child to the second woman and sent the first woman **back to her village with a sharp reprimand**. The child had been reunited with its rightful mother, who **embraced her and carried her off to their home**.

Exercise 4.5 Sample answers are provided.

The Joke

It was a cold day in **the northern regions**. Victor and Lara were school friends and decided **to enjoy the weather and the snow**. The snow was fresh and the hill was inviting, so they pulled their sled **up the steep slope**. When **Victor had placed the sled in the perfect position**, he sat behind Lara and **leaned close to her**. They went slowly at first, but **as the runners of the sled met an icy patch, they picked up speed** and **began a swift downward course**. They built up speed, and by now **the air was rushing around them**. Lara screamed with delight, and Victor **bellowed pretended words of fear**. He liked Lara a lot but was afraid **she had no real interest in him**. He wasn't shy, but **it**

was difficult to tell a girl how you felt. So, as they whizzed down the hill, he thought of a joke that **would let him say what he had in his heart**. As the air rushed past their ears, Victor leaned forward and whispered, "**I love you, Lara.**" Lara didn't seem to hear him, so **she leaned back against his face**. And he said in a hush, "I love you, Lara." She began to blush. She wasn't sure **what she had really heard**. Was it the wind? Was **it her own thoughts**? Was it Victor?

At the bottom of the hill, Victor looked at Lara, who **cast a questioning glance at him**. But he only smiled and **pulled the sled back to his home**. He could not say how he felt and only **spoke of the snow and the cold weather**.

They grew up, and Lara went **off to live in the capital**. While living there, she **married, raised a family, and in time buried her husband.** When she returned to her hometown many years later, she learned that Victor **had never married and still lived in the same old house**. They were both old now and **spending their final years with books and naps**. Lara decided it was time for **a little joke of her own.**

She saw Victor sitting **in a lawn chair** near a fence. She came up behind him on the other side of the fence and **listened to his restful breathing**. She peeked at him **over the fence and saw that he was old and frail**. And through a wide crack in one of the boards, Lara **whispered**, "**I love you, too, Victor.**" The wind was blowing hard and **rushing past his old ears**. The leaves were rustling above **his gray head**. Victor wasn't sure he had heard correctly. "**Is someone there**?" he asked, looking around. But there was no answer. Lara stood silently **and felt tears welling in her eyes**. Then she **leaned against the fence once more** and said in a whisper, "I love you, too, Victor."

The joke was on **both of them**.

Exercise 4.6 Sample answers are provided.

The Worst Day of My Life

Everyone has a bad day now and then. But I had the worst. It happened while I was visiting **some people in the city of Boston**. They were old friends of mine and had just moved to **the city from our hometown**. I loved spending time in a big city and was looking forward to **having some adventures there**.

I left my hometown around **sunup** and arrived **on the outskirts of Boston** around dusk. Before I found my friends' new house, my car **stalled on a road that led from the highway**. I thought I was out of gas, but **there was still plenty of fuel in the tank**. I wasn't sure what to do. I finally decided to **walk back toward the highway**. I thought I had seen a gas station there, but **when I arrived there, I only found a café and a saloon**. I thought I had better call my friends. I found a telephone booth and **dialed the new number they had given me**, but no one **answered and no answering machine picked up**.

Just as I began to walk back to my car, **it began to storm**. I was soaked to the skin by **the time I reached my car**. I tried starting my car again, but **the battery was apparently dead**. When it finally stopped raining, I got out of the car to **open the hood and check the engine**. As I stepped in front of the car, a truck zoomed by and **splashed me from head to toe**. My clothes were drenched again, and my face **was covered in thick mud**. I sputtered and cursed the truck, just as a car **plowed through a puddle and splashed me again**.

By now I was shivering from being so wet and from **the quickly falling temperature**. Late fall can be **extremely cold in Massachusetts**. I began to walk along the road in the direction of some bright lights. But I stepped in a puddle of mud and lost **my right shoe and sock**. I searched for **the shoe in the cold, black water**, but it was buried in mud. So I limped on, wearing **just one wet shoe**. Then the heel fell off of it, and now I was limping **both right and left**.

Finally I had some good luck. A taxi came by, and **I whistled in time to stop it**. Once I got inside the taxi, I began to warm up. I told the driver **to take me to my friends' address on Main Street**. I didn't realize how far it still was to their house. When I arrived at their house, **it was nearly midnight**. When I reached into my pocket, I discovered **I had lost my wallet out on the road somewhere**. I had no money! I was soaking wet! And I was tired!

I ran to my friends' door and rang the bell, but **there was no answer and there were no lights on**. Then I found a note for me taped to the door. It read, "**We were called away on an emergency. Check into a hotel**. We'll see you when we get back."

I sat on the wet porch and cried. It was the worst day of my life.

Exercise 4.7 Sample answers are provided.

The Desert

Jimmy was only eight when his parents **decided to leave the city to live in the country**. They moved to a large ranch near **a desert surrounded by a mountain range**. It was a wonderful place to live, but **a bit lonely at times**. Jimmy liked **the playground at his old school in the city** and thought the West was just **a lot of sand and too much open space**.

His little sister, Laura, was five and loved **the outdoors and the little wild animals**. She often played in the desert and **spent time looking at the strange plants and chasing the friendly creatures she found**. Jimmy warned her not to **go too far from the ranch**, but Laura **knew what she liked and did what she wanted.**

One day Laura **hiked toward an interesting-looking hill**, which was very far from their house. When she didn't come home for lunch, everyone **knew she was lost in the desert somewhere.** Jimmy was very worried. He got on his pony and **began galloping across the sand.** He rode as far as **the creek on the other side of the ranch.** Then he **rode through the field of gopher holes where his sister often played.** By three o'clock he had ridden **over acres of desert**, but he couldn't **find a trace of his sister.** He was ready to cry or even **just give up hope and go home.**

Then he saw it! It was a large **hill**, where Laura often **went to collect flowers.** He rode up to **the foot of the hill.** And there was Laura asleep next to **a patch of white daisies.** She didn't see **the rattlesnake**, which was crawling in her direction. Jimmy jumped from his pony and **moved silently toward his sister and the snake.** He took his lasso, swirled it overhead, and then **threw it above the snake.** He missed! He had to try again, so he **threw the rope carefully into the air, and it landed over the rattler's head**, and this time he **caught the snake and pulled it back into the brush** and saved his sister.

Exercise 4.8 Sample answers are provided.

The Hero

In winter it gets very cold in **northern Alaska**, because it's located near **the Arctic Circle.** A lot of snow falls to the ground, and a lot of **icicles hang from the rooflines of houses.**

Little Anna's house stays warm and **quite cozy**, because **it has thick log walls that protect everyone from the wind and cold.** There is a large fireplace in the dining room, where her grandfather **keeps a roaring fire day and night.** Anna loves **reading or playing near the fire**, while her grandfather **works his crossword puzzles or just dozes.**

One chilly December day, when **the temperature was falling quickly**, Grandfather noticed the fire **was getting low.** He went out to the barn and returned with **an enormous bundle of firewood.** Anna liked helping and **placed pieces of oak and maple in the fireplace.** Soon the fire **was large enough to heat the house properly again.** The dining room glowed with **dancing red lights.** The shadows on the walls **moved from side to side**, and everything in the house was **warm and cheerful.** Grandfather sat in his big, old armchair and soon **relaxed in the warmth coming from the hearth.** He put his feet on **a footstool and wiggled his toes**. Anna curled up on the floor under **a small blanket**. Everything was quiet and **perfect for a little snooze.**

Anna suddenly opened her eyes. Something was wrong! She smelled **the strong scent of smoke**! She saw **embers on the floor** and **flames on the drapes**! She jumped up and **looked around at the entire room**. The fire was no longer just in the fireplace. **The rugs and drapes were on fire**! Anna shook her grandfather, but **he was in a deep sleep**. She ran to the sink and **filled a pot with water**. She began throwing water **on the growing flames**. Finally the fire was out, and **the smoke had gone up the chimney**. When Grandfather awoke, he said, "**It looks like we need more wood for our fire**."

Anna just shook her head and smiled.

Exercise 4.9 Sample answers are provided.

The Pickpocket

It was a hot day, and **crowds of tourists wandered down Main Street**. People enjoyed holiday time like this and **looked in shop windows and enjoyed the warmth of a summer's afternoon**. It was a happy time for Mike because **it was the perfect time to acquire some money**. Mike knew there would be a lot of pockets that **were bulging with cash**. The crowds were enormous, and everyone **was busy looking around or just chatting**. Mike couldn't have been happier if **he had found the sidewalk littered with bills**. When **he thought the moment was right**, he walked slowly down the street and **waited for a tourist to come by**. Finally he saw **an elderly woman**, who **was very busy window shopping**. He came up behind her and carefully **reached into her purse**. The poor woman was aware of nothing and **continued to look at the goods in the window**. Her husband turned suddenly, but Mike **ran off into the crowd before he could stop him**. On the corner Mike saw **another preoccupied woman**, who **had a heavy purse over her shoulder**. Mike stood next to **her** and then **pretended to stumble**. He pulled out **a wallet from the woman's purse**. Mike smiled; he was very happy with himself and **walked briskly through the crowds of people**.

When he **saw a man with a bulging back pocket**, Mike decided **there was time for one more theft** and **soon was in possession of another wallet**. He got away that time and knew **he had been lucky**. But the policewoman **on the curb had been watching Mike**. Mike couldn't see **the officer observing him** and **tried still another theft**. When he slid his fingers into **a man's jacket pocket**, he was surprised **to feel a strong hand on his arm**. The policewoman had been watching him and **had run up to Mike as he stole the wallet**. Mike dropped **the**

wallet and tried **to make a run for it**. But the policewoman had **him firmly in her grip**; Mike was caught. He knew he couldn't get away now and said, "**I should have stopped with three**." The policewoman just laughed and replied, "**You never should have started at all**."

When they got to **the police station**, the officers there found **the other three wallets**. Trying to explain, Mike said, "**I found them**." But no one believed him. For the next few months Mike **would have time behind bars to think about his life as a pickpocket**.

Exercise 4.10 Sample answers are provided.

Laddy to the Rescue

During **the afternoon of a sunny day**, a seven-year-old girl decided to go for a walk. She went **across a meadow and into the woods** and soon realized that she was lost. She looked around her, but **nothing looked familiar**.

She began crying, and **she sat on a rock and wondered what to do**. But **she felt some hope when she saw a narrow clearing between the trees**. The little girl walked along the wide path bordered with **tall trees and thick shrubs**. Soon **it was getting dark**, and the little girl walked faster. There in the distance she could see **a small, dark cottage**. She opened the door and **stepped in cautiously**. There was a sudden, horrible noise, and **the girl turned and ran out the door and back to the woods**. She ran and ran and found herself alone in **a clearing surrounded by tall bushes**. She was terribly lonely and afraid, so **she sat on the ground and closed her eyes**. Cold and tired, she fell asleep near **a quietly bubbling stream**.

The little girl had a large, shaggy dog named Laddy. He was loyal to her and sensed that **she was in danger**. There was no way out of the house, so Laddy **jumped through a window, breaking the glass**. He ran to **the barn**; he looked in **the fields**, but Laddy couldn't **find his little mistress anywhere**. Suddenly there was a familiar scent on the ground. Laddy lowered his head and **followed the scent across the meadow**. He looked right and left. He barked **loudly into the air**. Then Laddy **searched through the woods** until he found **the little cottage**. But the strange little house was empty. Laddy looked around and **headed back to the woods**. Something caught his eye; Laddy suddenly saw **his mistress' blue shirt**. He jumped over some bushes and **headed straight for her**. A few moments later he saw **the little stream**, where the little girl **was sound asleep**. When she saw her dog standing over her, she said, "**You rescued me, Laddy**," and **the little girl kissed him several times**.

Laddy led his little mistress **out of the woods** and **across the meadow to her home**. Mother and Father were so relieved. And that night Laddy **had a hero's supper: steak with gravy**.

Exercise 4.11 Sample answers are provided.

The Day I Got Fired

I finally found a good job in **a factory not far from where I lived**. The company made electronics for **television and radio sets**. I was put on a line where **circuit boards were assembled**, and I had to **solder three particular circuits into the board**. The job was rather simple, and I believed I was doing well. Then they hired a new foreman, who **everyone said was really tough**. For some reason he didn't like me and often said, "**You're never going to last here**." I was afraid of him because he could **fire me at any time he wished**. And I needed my job. Without a job I **could lose my apartment or even my car**.

I knew I had to be careful around the foreman and **worked hard and long for him**. Then one day my car **broke down on the way to work**, and I arrived **nearly an hour late**. The foreman was **out of control** and began shouting at me. When I explained that **it wasn't entirely my fault**, he just laughed and **said it was my fault for buying an old car**. I went to my job and began **to put extra care into my work**. I worked hard and tried to **do everything perfectly**.

When lunchtime finally arrived, I sat at a table with **Mrs. Garcia, the accountant**. She was a really nice woman and told me **to treat the foreman with kid gloves**. But it wouldn't be easy to get along with him, because he **was a grumpy person and seemed to dislike me**.

After lunch I started soldering some new circuit boards. They had to be shipped to **Asia the next morning**. I was hurrying because **I wanted to get the work done on time**. But I worked too fast and ruined **seven of the ten sample boards**. The foreman was furious with me. He said, "**That was your last chance**!" Then he pointed at the door and shouted, "**Get out! You're fired**!"

I never went back there again. And now I have a better job, and my boss is a **very kind woman with a heart of gold**.

Exercise 4.12 Sample answers are provided.

The Blind Date

I had been going out with Barbara for more than **a year**. But we had some problems and decided **that our romance wasn't going anywhere**. We're still friends, and we often get together to **chat over a glass of wine**.

Several months went by after we broke up, and I **realized I was spending too much time at home**. It was getting boring sitting at home and **watching TV or washing clothes and doing chores**. Then my friend Bill suggested I go out on a blind date. I had never **dated anyone I didn't know well** and wasn't sure that a blind date **would be something I could tolerate**. But I agreed, and Bill **said he knew someone perfect for me.**

He arranged for me to meet **his friend Angela over dinner**. She was a friend of his from work. He said she **was very bright and outgoing** and **was the nicest woman he ever met**. I like women who **are personable**, so I was interested to meet her. At eight P.M. on Saturday, I left home and **drove to a little café on the edge of town**. I went in and took a seat near **a window so I could watch for her**. About ten minutes later a woman who **looked very attractive in her pink dress** came in and began to look around. I knew **it was Angela, my blind date.**

She took a seat across from me and said, "**Bill told me you were nice looking, and he was right**." I was flattered because she **was one of the most beautiful women I had ever seen**. We chatted a while and then ordered some dinner. She had quite an appetite and **ate everything on her plate**. I had never seen a woman eat so much. "I like to cook," she finally said, "and I **love to eat everything I cook**."

The evening went by quickly because **we had a lot to talk about and we were enjoying ourselves**. I didn't think I could fall in love so fast, but **I was falling for Angela very quickly**. We went out several times during the next **several months**, and when spring came we were inseparable. I finally bought **an engagement ring**, and on June first I **asked her to marry me**. To my amazement she immediately said, "**I've been waiting to hear that question a long time. Yes.**"

After a yearlong engagement, we **were married in a big wedding held at Bill's house**. Now we have a house and **two little children** and a third on the way. I have never been happier and believe that **you never know when you'll find the one you love.**

Who could have known that a blind date **would bring me such happiness**.

Exercise 4.13 Sample answers are provided.

No More Used Cars!

Buying a new car is expensive. That's why I **always had a used car**. I would love to own a new car, but for now **I am living on a budget and have to drive an older car**. Last winter my old car finally died. I tried to start it, but **it had no**

more life left in it. I sold it for junk and went to buy **something a little newer and more reliable**.

I had seen the Johnson's Pre-Owned Vehicles lot **on my way to work** and decided to stop there to **check out the cars**. Some of the cars were just too old, and others **too expensive for my budget**. I had to make a compromise between **how new the car was** and **how much it cost**. I finally found a **compact two-door sedan** with a little rust on it, but it seemed to run **rather well**.

I paid Mr. Johnson with a check, signed **the necessary documents**, and drove home **in my "new" little car**. I was rather proud of my new vehicle. It looked **rather sporty** and sounded **like a finely tuned machine**. My brother was impressed with my purchase and said, "**This is the best car you've ever had**." But my father was skeptical. He laughed and said to me, "Used cars **are a special breed of wild animal. Watch out**."

My "new" car ran well for a long time. Then on a very cold morning in January, I went to the garage and **tried to start it**. But the car **was ice-cold, and the engine wouldn't turn over**. It was frustrating. It just wouldn't start. My brother came out to the garage and **jumped my battery from his car**. Finally the motor was running, and I **was on my way to my job**. I arrived at work late and explained that **my new car had had a problem**.

When five o'clock came and I was ready **to head for home**, I went out to the parking lot to start my car. And again **it wouldn't start**. Now I was mad. Really mad! I looked at that car and shouted, "**You're nothing but a piece of junk**!" Naturally, the car couldn't understand what I said and just **sat in the parking lot without moving**. One of my coworkers was watching me and **laughed at how silly I looked**. It was pretty embarrassing.

It took half an hour to start that car, but it **finally turned over, and I could leave work**. I wish it had never started. Two blocks from work the engine **froze up**, and I was stuck in the middle of the street. I got it started again, and two blocks later the radiator **began to overflow**. That old car stalled five times on the way home.

When I finally arrived there, my family was **waiting for me at the supper table**. They knew something was wrong with my car because **my clothes were dirty and there was anger in my face**. My father laughed again and said, "Don't buy a used car unless **you are a mechanic or own an automobile parts store**." I knew he was right and got a tune-up the next day.

My car wasn't perfect after that, but it **got me to work and home again**. And I learned a lesson: if you're going to buy a used car, you had better **check**

it out carefully. As for me, I hope to get rich and never **have to drive a piece of junk again**.

Exercise 4.14 Sample answers are provided.

Computers Can Be Dumb

I was always afraid of computers. They **were very mysterious to me** and made me feel **like I was just a dumb human**. Of course, they are just machines and can't **think like a human**. But I always felt that they were trying to make me look foolish.

When I got a job in a warehouse, I had to learn **to enter data in a computer**. It's not what I wanted to do, but it was part of the job. So I reluctantly **got the training and began working with the computer**. In time, I thought I had mastered **the skills for using the machine**, but the truth was that the computer **really had a mind of its own**. As I gained more experience, the computer seemed to make more mistakes. I'd type in one number, and the computer **would put in something completely different**. I complained to my boss that the computer I was using **was changing my inputs**. He laughed and told me to **remember that a computer is only as smart as the person running it**.

Then for a few weeks everything went fine. I **gave my inputs**, and the computer **recorded them properly in a file**. But then it began. I'd come to work and turn on the computer, and **the screen would be filled with crazy words and numbers**. I couldn't believe my eyes. How could **something so incredible** happen? Where did **all the strange data** come from? I didn't type in those things. I knew it was the computer trying **to make me look bad**.

Finally my boss came to me with some complaints from management. He asked, "**Why are you putting so many wrong numbers into the files**?" I said it wasn't my fault, and once again he laughed and said, "**Don't try to blame your mistakes on the computer**." No one believed me. Why would anyone believe that **a machine was out to destroy me**? It was too incredible.

Then I got the news. The manager sent word to my boss that **my work was unacceptable**. The next day I got my final paycheck. My boss said my work had too many mistakes and **I had to be let go**. He told me to **pick up my last check and leave**. I went home and felt **like a complete fool**.

Two days later I got a telephone call. It was the manager. He said that **there had been a terrible mistake** and that I could have my job back. It turned out that the computer **was making the mistakes all along**; it had a defective motherboard. I was so happy that I **danced around the kitchen with the phone in my hand**.

I returned to work the next day and sat down to a new computer. This one was friendly, and we **became a real team immediately**.

Exercise 4.15 Sample answers are provided.

How I Became a Millionaire

Many people dream about becoming rich and living **the life of a king or queen**. They hope they'll win **a lottery** or inherit **a fortune**. But it doesn't work out that way for most.

One morning I got out of bed and ran down the stairs to get the mail. I had a feeling that **this was going to be my lucky day**. And I was right. Among the letters I found was **one from the state lottery commission**. It stated that I **was the latest big winner**. I couldn't believe my eyes. I had won **two million dollars**! I was a millionaire!

I called my best friend, Anna, who **screamed when I told her the news**. She was as excited as I was and **ran over to my house in her robe**. She asked, "**What are you going to do now that you're rich**?" And she asked, "**What are you going to spend all that money on**?" I didn't know the answer. Where do you begin to spend money, when **you never had a lot of money to spend before**? I was new at this, but I **knew I would catch on fast**. You learn some things fast.

Anna and I went downtown, but not on the bus. We **took a cab**, and on the way home I rented **a stretch limousine**. I felt like a queen. I could afford anything I wanted, and I wanted **to buy the best of everything**. But Anna was wiser than me. She suggested **I invest some of the money** and **set up a budget for the rest**. I realized that was smart and decided I would put some money **in a savings account**. But I would spend the rest on **luxuries of every kind**. Why not? I was a millionaire!

I bought several new dresses for myself, and for Anna **I bought a watch, two bracelets, and a dress for evening wear**. She was elated and said, "**I'm going to look like a queen in these**." We both loved shoes, so **we spent three hours trying on shoes**. And I stocked up on **perfume** and **a variety of lingerie**. I was on a buying spree, and **nothing was going to stop me**.

But something did stop me. It didn't seem possible. It **didn't seem like the right way to end things**. I was being tricked. Fate had **cheated me**. It wasn't fair, and I lowered my head **and wept loudly**. It wasn't fair!

I had been a millionaire for **only a short time**. Just like so many others, I had only dreamed it. My wealth was just **a wish come true in my sleep**.

Exercise 5.1 Sample completions are provided.

August 1, 2004

3111 West Main Street
Johnstown, IL 60622

Dear Bill,

I finally bought the new car I've been talking about. I was able to get a loan from my local bank, and together with what I've saved, I was able to get the car. It is bright red and looks fantastic.

When fall comes, I want to take a drive to New England. I've heard that the autumn foliage is spectacular. And it will be a good opportunity to try out my new car. Maybe you'll have the time to come with me.

I had hoped to ask my brother to join me on the trip, but he was in a skiing accident last winter, and his leg hasn't yet healed properly. Although he's still on crutches, he's able to go to work.

Yours truly,
Jim

Exercise 5.2 Sample completions are provided.

October 5, 2003

1199 Oak Street
Johnstown, IL 60622

My Dear Barbara,

You may have heard by now that I lost some money recently. What you probably don't know is that it was a whole month's salary. When I got my monthly paycheck, I cashed it at my bank. Then I put the money in my purse and headed for home, but somehow I left my purse on the bus. I know it was a careless and stupid thing to do.

Yesterday a little boy came to my door and asked if I had lost anything recently. I told him I had lost my purse and described it to him. He just looked at me for a moment.

Then he pulled my purse from behind his back and handed it to me. Everything was in it: my wallet, my credit cards, my driver's license, and all my money. I was so relieved that I gave the boy fifty dollars. It's good to know that there are nice people in the world.

Yours,
Aunt Mary

Exercise 5.3 Sample completions are provided.

November 10, 2004

111 James Lane
Johnstown, IL 60622

Dear Mr. Brown,

It's been more than two months since I moved to my new apartment, so I wanted to contact you with the news that I'm finally settled. I have two bedrooms and one bath, and the kitchen is enormous. But as much as I like my new place, I still miss the cozy place I rented from you.

I'm still adjusting to living in such a small town. It seems that everyone knows everyone here. The clerk at the grocery store already calls me by my first name, and my next-door neighbor has had me over for lunch twice. It's very pleasant here, but I think I prefer a big city.

However, I really like my job. And if I get a raise and a promotion next year, I'd like to buy a house. If I had one more bedroom, my mother could move in with me, and I'd still have a bedroom to use as an office.

Sincerely Yours,
Jane Smith

Exercise 5.5 Sample completions are provided.

August 7, 2004

3111 West Main Street
Johnstown, IL 60622
(311) 555-1234

James Jones, Manager
Specialty Electronics
5566 North Fuller Avenue
Johnstown, IL 60633

Subject: Defective CD Player

Dear Mr. Jones:

I have been a customer of your store for more than three years. On August 1 I purchased a Crown CD player (model A-2003) from you for $155.95.

From the first moment when I tried to use the CD player, it was clear that something was wrong with it. The power light did not come on. The buttons caused nothing to work. In short, the product is defective.

I have heard good things about this brand of CD player and would prefer to have a replacement for it. If that is not possible, please arrange for a refund of my money. A copy of my receipt is enclosed. I can be contacted at the above address or phone number.

Thank you.

Sincerely,

Jim Brown

Enclosure (1)

Exercise 5.6 Sample completions are provided.

July 10, 2004

5590 West Oak Avenue
Johnstown, IL 60644
(311) 555-1234

Ms. Anne Smith
Acme Manufacturing
24 Workman Lane
Johnstown, IL 60651

Subject: Job Opportunities

Dear Ms. Smith:

I am a twenty-five-year-old machinist with four years' experience in a variety of areas of tooling. I understand that you are hiring new people, and I should like to make application with your company.

I have references from my two previous employers and a complete résumé of my experience and salary history. I have enclosed them with this letter.

I am available to begin work at the earliest possible date. At your convenience, I shall be happy to come in for an interview.

Thank you for your consideration. I look forward to hearing from you in the near future.

Sincerely yours,

Michelle Miller

Enclosures (3)

Exercise 5.7 Sample completions are provided.

December 30, 2004

5590 West Oak Avenue
Johnstown, IL 60644
(311) 555-1234

Sloan Management Co.
8033 Grove Avenue
Johnstown, IL 60691

Attention: Properties Manager

Subject: Lack of Heat

I have been a tenant in your building at 5590 West Oak Avenue, Apartment 3A, for ten months. Since December 21 there has been little or no heat in my apartment. I have called your office four times, but I have only reached an answering machine.

At this cold time of year and in the flu season, the lack of heat is a health risk to my two small children and me. We must have adequate heat immediately. I have been told that the problem is that the radiators have to be bled to allow the heat to flow properly.

Please make the radiator repairs as soon as possible. If this is not done within four days, I shall contact the city's department of health and make a complaint.

Sincerely,

Mrs. Jane Brown

Exercise 6.1 *The Car I've Always Wanted*

My old car needed a paint job and had bad brakes. It was time to buy a newer car, something more modern and up-to-date. I went to the largest dealership on Main Street and received help from one of the salesmen. He showed me all the latest models. But everything was so expensive.

Finally I saw a dark blue convertible on the far end of the lot. It was a two-year-old Chevy, and it was in great condition. The price was right, so the salesman drew up the papers, I gladly signed, and a half hour later I drove off the lot in my "almost new" Chevy.

But getting this car hasn't been the best idea. My brother always wants to borrow it. My girlfriend always wants to drive it. And I only get to use it when I go to work and when the car needs gas.

Exercise 6.2 *Death Came for a Visit*

My great-grandfather was ninety-two years old and suffering from a long illness. We knew he would pass away soon, but that's not easy even if someone is old. His last wish was to have the entire family with him at the end. So on a cold day that seemed designed for our impending loss, we gathered at his bedside.

Aunt Louise, who was Great-grandfather's youngest sister, sat next to him. She said quiet, comforting words to him, but I doubt he heard her. Then something that no one had expected happened. Great-grandfather opened his eyes and seemed to look around.

"It's time," he said quietly. Then he shut his eyes and slipped into his eternal sleep.

Although I felt a certain sadness, I was relieved to know that he was finally released from his illness. Death isn't easy, but it's something we all must endure.

Exercise 6.3 *The Most Unforgettable Day*

The most amazing thing happened one day when I was at the beach. I have often spent time at the seashore, but this time it was something special. I was enjoying myself, watching the waves and the surf, when I found a bottle in the sand. I have never gone looking for treasure, but the bottle was the vehicle that sent me on such a course.

The bottle itself was nothing special: it was small and made of brown glass. But inside was a note with just a few words: "Look beneath the cliffs." Because of those four simple words, I began a quest that went on for two weeks.

I searched beneath every cliff along the shoreline. I hunted in caves and on rocky slopes. But I didn't find any treasure. Then one evening at sunset, I sat beneath a jagged cliff and peered out over the sea. That's when I found my treasure: the most beautiful sunset I had ever seen. It was unforgettable and gave me a happiness I remember to this day.

Exercise 6.4 *Peace or War*

It must have been difficult for the Founding Fathers to choose in favor of revolution and war against England. Such a step was surely taken with great fear. Everything could be lost if the war ended in favor of England. And thousands of men, women, and children from all the colonies would suffer or even die.

But the fight for freedom was just, and that made the war inevitable. The American colonists had to take command of their own liberty or perish in the process. When negotiations and diplomacy failed, it was time to act.

No war is good. It means death and destruction for so many, but perhaps the good that is derived after the war is justification enough for it. At least that was so in the case of the American Revolution.

Exercise 6.5 *A Wedding*

My cousin, Anne, and her fiancé were married several years ago. Instead of a June wedding, they got married in late October. The vows they spoke were simple but beautiful. Everyone cried, especially Anne's new mother-in-law.

The reception Anne's parents arranged was held in a large hall in the city. Guests enjoyed dancing and wonderful food. But instead of an open bar, each table was provided with several bottles of champagne. Everyone celebrated happily.

Around midnight the bride and groom slipped away. The following morning they left for their honeymoon in Jamaica.

Next October they will have been married for ten years.

Exercise 6.6 *Credit Cards*

If I had known then what I know now about credit cards, I never would have signed up for one. I thought a credit card would give me freedom and allow me to enjoy the things that were out of my grasp financially. But that's not the way it turned out.

I found myself buying things I didn't need. If I saw a dress I liked, I would buy it, even if I thought it was too expensive. Little by little my debt grew, and with the high interest rate, I found that I couldn't pay my bills.

One day I went to an ATM to get some money, and I discovered that my credit card didn't work. I had spent too much, and I owed too much. But I had finally learned my lesson. I cut up the card and got a second job. It took two years, but I'm finally out of debt. And I don't want another credit card.

Exercise 6.7 *I Need a Vacation*

At summer's end last year, I was exhausted. I needed time away from work. So I went to a travel agent to arrange a trip someplace quiet and relaxing. The agent suggested Sanibel Island in Florida.

"Are you going to be traveling alone?" she asked me.

That was the first time I had thought about it. I didn't want to vacation alone. My brother's wife was visiting her mother for a while, so I invited him to join me. But he couldn't get away from work. So I asked my friend Bill. But Bill's job required him to travel later in the fall.

Then I realized that it wasn't important where I spent my vacation time. It was more important to be with the people I care about. I called the travel agent and told her that I wouldn't be taking a trip anywhere that year. I'm going to spend my free time with family and friends instead.

Exercise 6.8 *The Person I Love Most*

Maria became my wife just two years ago. I love her so much and know that she loves me, too. Our relationship is so strong and based on mutual affection and respect. We both admitted long ago that we had found in one another our soul mates.

It's so important to have someone that you love so much. Everyone needs someone that he can talk to and confide in. It's a form of comfort and security. And my Maria is all of that.

Our love is real and forever. And that kind of love is hard to find. But when you do find it, you have to nurture it and care for it like a delicate flower. If you do, it will go on and on.

Exercise 6.9 *If I Had a Million Dollars*

Who would have believed it? I won a million dollars in the lottery. Lots of people have been taken in by the notion that they'll strike it rich someday. But it really happened to me. When it does, what do you do with all that money?

The answer isn't so easy. For years I have been plagued by the idea that having lots of money would solve all my problems. But money just adds to the problems. In addition to taxes, there are friends and relatives, all of whom need a loan. Everybody seems to want something from you. You begin to feel that people only like you for your wealth.

I foolishly went on a buying spree. I bought three cars, a new house, a boat, and a closet full of clothes for every season. How could I have been so stupid? The money was soon gone, and I was back at my old job. But I had learned an important and very old lesson: money doesn't always buy happiness.

Exercise 6.10 *My First Job*

I sometimes have to laugh when I think about my first job. I was sixteen years old and believed that "a man" of that advanced age ought to earn his own keep. So I got a job sweeping up in a hardware store. I dusted shelves, swept floors, and cleaned toilets. It was so boring.

One day Mr. Jones, the owner of the store, said I had to help customers because he was short-handed. I was glad to do it and to leave my broom in the back room.

But there was a problem. I wasn't able to help anybody. I didn't know a dead bolt from a coping saw. I didn't know that nails came in different sizes, and all I did was frustrate Mr. Jones' customers.

At the end of the week I got my paycheck and a little yellow slip that said I was fired. It was a relief.